OIL TRADING 101

Mastering the Oil Market: CFDs, Futures & Options

Usiere Uko

Copyright © 2024 Usiere Uko

All Rrghts reserved.

No part of this publication may be reproduced, distributed, or transmitted in any form or by any means, including photocopying, recording, or other electronic or mechanical methods, without the prior written permission of the publisher, except in the case of brief quotations embodied in critical reviews and certain other noncommercial uses permitted by copyright law.
This publication is designed to provide accurate and authoritative information in regard to the subject matter covered. It is sold with the understanding that the publisher is not engaged in rendering legal, accounting, or other professional services. If legal advice or other expert assistance is required, the services of a competent professional should be sought.
The author and publisher shall not be liable for any loss of profit or any other commercial damages, including but not limited to special, incidental, consequential, or other damages.

ISBN-13: 979-8-332-86151-2

FIRST EDITION

...To new frontiers, learning and growing

CONTENTS

Title Page
Copyright
Dedication
INTRODUCTION
PART 1: INTRODUCTION TO OIL TRADING   1
Chapter 1: Overview of the Oil Market   2
Chapter 2: Importance of Oil in the Global Economy   5
Chapter 3: Different Types of Oil   8
PART 2: FUNDAMENTALS OF OIL TRADING   14
Chapter 4: Supply and Demand Dynamics   15
Chapter 5: Key Players in the Oil Market   21
Chapter 6: Impact of Geopolitical Events   25
PART 3: OIL MARKET INSTRUMENTS   29
Chapter 7: Understanding Oil CFDs   30
Chapter 8: Introduction to Oil Futures   35
Chapter 9: Basics of Oil Options   42
PART 4: MARKET ANALYSIS TECHNIQUES   48
Chapter 10: Fundamental Analysis for Oil Trading   49
Chapter 11: Technical Analysis: Charts and Indicators 55
Chapter 12: Sentiment Analysis in Oil Trading   66
PART 5: TRADING PLATFORMS AND TOOLS   72

Chapter 13: Choosing the Right Trading Platform	73
Chapter 14: Essential Tools for Oil Traders	80
Chapter 15: Using Trading Software and Apps	87
PART 6: DEVELOPING A TRADING STRATEGY	95
Chapter 16: Setting Trading Goals	96
Chapter 17: Risk Management and Position Sizing	105
Chapter 18: Creating a Trading Plan	114
PART 7: EXECUTING TRADES	123
Chapter 19: Placing Orders	124
Chapter 20: Understanding Spreads and Leverage	131
Chapter 21: Managing Open Positions	138
PART 8: ADVANCED TRADING STRATEGIES	146
Chapter 22: Spread Trading in Oil Markets	147
Chapter 23: Hedging with Futures and Options	156
Chapter 24: Swing Trading and Day Trading Techniques	166
PART 9: RISK MANAGEMENT AND PSYCHOLOGY	173
Chapter 25: Identifying and Mitigating Risks	174
Chapter 26: Dealing with Market Volatility	184
Chapter 27: Psychological Aspects of Trading: Discipline and Emotions	192
PART 10: FUTURE TRENDS IN OIL TRADING	202
Chapter 28: Impact of Renewable Energy on Oil Markets	203
Chapter 29: Technological Advancements in Trading	211
PART 11: RESOURCES AND FURTHER READING	216
Chapter 30: Recommended Resources	217
Chapter 31: Industry Reports and Market Data Sources	220
PART 12: CONCLUSION AND NEXT STEPS	223
Chapter 32: Recap of Key Concepts	224

Chapter 33: Final Tips for Aspiring Oil Traders	228
Chapter 34: Encouragement for Continuous Learning	233
About The Author	237
Books In This Series	239
Books By This Author	241

INTRODUCTION

UNDERSTANDING THE BASICS OF TRADING THE OIL MARKET, CFDS, FUTURES AND OPTIONS

Welcome to ***Oil Trading 101: Understanding the Basics of Trading the Oil Market, CFDs, Futures, and Options.*** This book is your essential guide to navigating the intricate and influential world of oil trading. Whether you're a novice exploring the fundamentals or a seasoned trader looking to refine your strategies, this comprehensive introduction equips you with the knowledge and tools necessary to succeed in this dynamic sector.

UNVEILING THE FOUNDATIONS

The global oil market is a cornerstone of the global economy, driven by complex factors including geopolitical events, supply-demand dynamics, and technological advancements. In this book, we embark on a journey to unravel the fundamentals of oil trading:

Market Dynamics: We begin by exploring the fundamental workings of the oil market, including the types of oil traded, key market influencers, and the roles of major players like OPEC and non-OPEC nations.

Financial Instruments: From traditional futures and options to modern Contracts for Difference (CFDs), we delve into the various instruments available for trading oil, discussing their uses, risks, and strategic applications.

MASTERING TRADING TECHNIQUES

Understanding the nuances of trading techniques is crucial for success in oil markets:

Analytical Approaches: We cover essential techniques such as fundamental analysis, technical indicators, and sentiment analysis, empowering you to interpret market data and make informed trading decisions.

Risk Management: Effective risk management is central to sustainable trading. We provide insights into minimizing risks, setting achievable trading goals, and developing resilient risk management strategies.

EMBRACING INNOVATION

In today's digital age, technological advancements are revolutionizing trading practices:

Integration of Technology: Explore the integration of algorithmic trading, artificial intelligence, and big data analytics, uncovering how these innovations enhance trading efficiency and strategy formulation.

YOUR JOURNEY BEGINS HERE

As you embark on your journey through **Oil Trading 101**, anticipate gaining a solid understanding of global energy markets, refining your trading acumen, and cultivating a strategic approach to achieving your financial objectives. Each chapter is crafted to offer practical insights, real-world examples, and actionable advice, ensuring you emerge equipped to navigate the complexities of oil trading confidently.

Prepare to embark on an enriching learning experience in oil trading. Let's explore and master the fundamentals together.

PART 1: INTRODUCTION TO OIL TRADING

CHAPTER 1: OVERVIEW OF THE OIL MARKET

Oil is often referred to as the lifeblood of the global economy. It powers industries, fuels transportation, and plays a critical role in the production of various goods. Understanding the oil market is essential for anyone interested in trading oil or its derivatives, such as CFDs, futures, and options.

The oil market is vast and complex, influenced by a myriad of factors including geopolitical events, economic conditions, and technological advancements. This chapter provides an overview of the oil market, its key components, and the fundamental dynamics that drive it.

THE IMPORTANCE OF OIL IN THE GLOBAL ECONOMY

Oil is a crucial energy source, accounting for a significant portion of the world's energy consumption. It is used to produce gasoline, diesel, jet fuel, heating oil, and various petrochemicals. The global demand for oil affects not only the energy sector but also has broader economic implications, influencing inflation, trade balances, and economic growth.

Major industries, from transportation to manufacturing, rely heavily on oil. The price of oil, therefore, has a direct impact on the cost of goods and services worldwide. Understanding how the oil market operates can provide valuable insights into broader economic trends and potential investment opportunities.

KEY PLAYERS IN THE OIL MARKET

The oil market is composed of a variety of participants, each playing a unique role. Key players include:

Producers: These are countries and companies that extract crude oil from the ground. Major oil-producing countries include Saudi Arabia, Russia, the United States, and members of the Organization of the Petroleum Exporting Countries (OPEC).

Consumers: These are countries and industries that consume oil. The largest oil-consuming countries are the United States, China, and India, where demand for energy to fuel economic growth is high.

Traders: These are individuals and institutions that buy and sell oil and its derivatives in the financial markets. Traders seek to profit from price movements by speculating on future prices or hedging against price risks.

Refiners: These companies process crude oil into refined products like gasoline, diesel, and jet fuel. They play a crucial role in the supply chain, determining the availability of different petroleum products.

Regulatory Bodies: Organizations like the International Energy Agency (IEA) and national governments regulate the oil industry, setting policies that impact production, consumption, and trading practices.

FACTORS INFLUENCING OIL PRICES

Oil prices are influenced by a complex interplay of factors, including:

Supply and Demand: The fundamental driver of oil prices is the balance between supply and demand. An oversupply can lead to lower prices, while high demand can drive prices up.

Geopolitical Events: Political instability, conflicts, and decisions by major oil-producing countries can significantly impact oil prices. For example, production cuts by OPEC can lead to higher prices, while increased production can lead to lower prices.

Economic Indicators: Global economic health, indicated by metrics such as GDP growth, unemployment rates, and industrial production, affects oil demand and prices.

Currency Fluctuations: Oil is typically traded in US dollars, so fluctuations in the value of the dollar can impact oil prices. A weaker dollar makes oil cheaper for holders of other currencies, potentially increasing demand and prices.

Technological Advances: Innovations in extraction and production technologies, such as hydraulic fracturing (fracking) and deep-water drilling, can alter the supply landscape and influence prices.

Weather and Natural Disasters: Severe weather conditions and natural disasters can disrupt oil production and supply chains, leading to price volatility.

Understanding the oil market is fundamental for anyone looking to trade oil or its derivatives. By grasping the basics of how the oil market operates and recognizing the key players and types of crude oil, aspiring traders can build a solid foundation for their trading journey.

CHAPTER 2: IMPORTANCE OF OIL IN THE GLOBAL ECONOMY

Oil is a critical component of the global economy, influencing various sectors and driving economic growth. Its significance extends beyond being a primary energy source; oil plays a pivotal role in manufacturing, transportation, and international trade. Understanding the multifaceted importance of oil is essential for traders and investors aiming to navigate the oil market effectively.

ENERGY SOURCE AND ECONOMIC DRIVER

Oil is a major source of energy, accounting for about one-third of global energy consumption. It fuels transportation systems, powers industries, and provides heating and electricity. The availability and price of oil directly affect economic activities and growth rates. Lower oil prices can reduce transportation and production costs, leading to lower consumer prices and stimulating economic growth. Conversely, higher oil prices can increase costs, contributing to inflation and potentially slowing economic growth.

TRANSPORTATION AND MOBILITY

The transportation sector is heavily dependent on oil. Gasoline, diesel, and jet fuel, all derived from crude oil, power cars, trucks, airplanes, and ships. Efficient and affordable transportation is crucial for global trade and commerce, enabling the movement of goods and people. Fluctuations in oil prices can significantly impact transportation costs, affecting supply chains and the prices of goods and services worldwide.

INDUSTRIAL AND MANUFACTURING USES

Oil is a key input in various industrial and manufacturing processes. Petrochemicals derived from oil are used to produce plastics, fertilizers, pharmaceuticals, and synthetic materials. The availability and cost of oil and its derivatives influence the production costs and pricing of a wide range of products. Industries such as chemicals, construction, and agriculture rely on oil-based materials, making oil a vital component of industrial production.

IMPACT ON TRADE BALANCES AND NATIONAL ECONOMIES

Oil exports and imports play a significant role in the trade balances of many countries. Oil-exporting nations, such as Saudi Arabia, Russia, and Venezuela, derive a substantial portion of their revenues from oil exports. These revenues are crucial for funding government expenditures and development projects. Conversely, oil-importing countries, such as Japan, India, and many European nations, face significant costs associated with importing oil to meet their energy needs.

Changes in oil prices can alter trade balances, impacting national economies. A rise in oil prices benefits oil-exporting countries by increasing their export revenues, while oil-importing countries face higher import costs, potentially leading to trade deficits and economic challenges.

GEOPOLITICAL INFLUENCE AND STRATEGIC IMPORTANCE

Oil is not just an economic commodity; it is also a strategic resource with significant geopolitical implications. Control over oil resources and supply routes has historically been a source of power and influence. Countries with abundant oil reserves often wield considerable geopolitical influence, shaping global energy policies and international relations.

Geopolitical events, such as conflicts in oil-producing regions, sanctions, and diplomatic negotiations, can disrupt oil supplies and cause price volatility. For example, tensions in the Middle East, home to a substantial portion of the world's oil reserves, can lead to supply disruptions and sharp price increases, affecting the global economy.

ENVIRONMENTAL AND SUSTAINABILITY CONCERNS

While oil is a critical economic driver, its extraction, production, and consumption have significant environmental impacts. Oil spills, air pollution, and greenhouse gas emissions associated with oil use contribute to environmental degradation and climate change. The transition to renewable energy sources and the development of sustainable practices are gaining momentum as the world seeks to reduce its dependence on fossil fuels and mitigate environmental impacts.

Efforts to balance economic growth with environmental sustainability are influencing global energy policies and investment strategies. The shift towards cleaner energy sources and technologies presents both challenges and opportunities for the oil industry and traders.

The importance of oil in the global economy cannot be overstated. As a primary energy source, it fuels transportation, powers industries, and drives economic growth. Oil's influence extends to trade balances, geopolitical relations, and environmental sustainability.

Understanding the multifaceted role of oil is crucial for anyone involved in the oil market, from traders and investors to policymakers and industry stakeholders.

CHAPTER 3: DIFFERENT TYPES OF OIL

Crude oil is not a uniform commodity; it varies significantly in composition and quality, leading to different classifications and benchmarks in the market. Understanding the types of oil and their characteristics is crucial for traders as it affects pricing, trading strategies, and market analysis.

This chapter explores the major types of crude oil, focusing on Brent Crude and West Texas Intermediate (WTI), as well as other important grades.

CLASSIFICATION OF CRUDE OIL

Crude oil is classified based on its physical and chemical properties. The two primary factors are:

Density (API Gravity): Measured by the American Petroleum Institute (API) gravity scale, it indicates how heavy or light the oil is compared to water. Higher API gravity means lighter oil.

Sulfur Content: Crude oil can be either "sweet" or "sour" based on its sulfur content. Sweet crude has low sulfur content, while sour crude has high sulfur content.

These properties determine the quality of the crude oil and its suitability for refining into various products. Light, sweet crude oils are generally more desirable because they produce a higher yield of valuable products like gasoline and diesel.

BRENT CRUDE

Brent Crude stands as one of the paramount benchmarks in the global oil market, renowned for its consistent quality and widespread usage in pricing crude oil. Sourced primarily from the North Sea, this crude oil is characterized by its lightness and sweet nature, making it highly desirable for refining into gasoline and diesel fuels.

Location: Extracted from oil fields in the North Sea, specifically between the Shetland Islands and Norway.

API Gravity: Approximately 38.06, indicating its relatively light density.

Sulfur Content: About 0.37%, classified as low sulfur or "sweet" crude, which reduces refining costs.

Regional Usage: Brent Crude serves as a pivotal pricing benchmark for oil consumed across Europe, Africa, and the Middle East, influencing the pricing of refined products in these regions.

Global Benchmark: It serves as a reference for pricing over two-thirds of the world's traded oil, establishing a baseline for global oil pricing mechanisms.

Price Indicator: The price of Brent Crude is widely monitored and reported globally, making it a key indicator of international oil market trends and sentiments.

Market Platform: Brent Crude futures are predominantly traded on the Intercontinental Exchange (ICE), offering liquidity and transparency to traders and investors.

Market Influence: Its status as a benchmark ensures that fluctuations in Brent Crude prices can directly impact global oil prices, influencing decisions across the energy sector and financial markets.

WEST TEXAS INTERMEDIATE (WTI)

West Texas Intermediate (WTI) holds a pivotal position as a leading benchmark in the global oil market, renowned for its premium quality and widespread use in pricing crude oil. Originating from fields primarily in Texas and surrounding states within the United States, WTI is distinguished by its lightness and sweet characteristics, making it highly desirable for refining into gasoline and other high-demand products.

Location: Produced from oil fields predominantly in Texas, as well as parts of Oklahoma, Kansas, and New Mexico.

API Gravity: Approximately 39.6, indicating its relatively light density, which simplifies refining processes.

Sulfur Content: About 0.24%, categorizing it as low sulfur or "sweet" crude, resulting in reduced refining costs and environmental impact.

Primary Benchmark: WTI serves as the primary benchmark for oil prices in North America, influencing the pricing of crude oil and refined products across the continent.

Market Influence: It is widely used by traders, refineries, and financial institutions as a key indicator of oil prices in the United States, reflecting market sentiment and economic conditions.

Price Dynamics: Typically priced slightly lower than Brent Crude due to its inland location, which necessitates higher transportation costs to reach global markets.

Market Platform: WTI futures contracts are predominantly traded on the New York Mercantile Exchange (NYMEX), providing a transparent and liquid market environment for investors and traders.

Market Utilization: Its status as a benchmark ensures that fluctuations in WTI prices have a direct impact on crude oil prices across North America, influencing strategic decisions within the energy sector and financial markets.

OTHER NOTABLE CRUDE OILS

DUBAI CRUDE

Location: Dubai, United Arab Emirates (Middle East)
API Gravity: Approximately 31
Sulfur Content: About 2%

Regional Benchmark: Dubai Crude serves as a benchmark for pricing oil in the Persian Gulf region, reflecting market dynamics and influencing pricing strategies in the Middle East.

Heavy Crude: With a lower API gravity and higher sulfur content compared to Brent and WTI, Dubai Crude is typically heavier and sourer, requiring more complex refining processes.

OPEC REFERENCE BASKET

Composition: A weighted average of crude oils from various OPEC member countries.

OPEC Benchmark: The OPEC Reference Basket provides a comprehensive benchmark for monitoring OPEC's oil production and pricing policies.

Market Indicator: It serves as a reference point for understanding price trends within OPEC member states and the organization's influence on global oil markets.

OTHER REGIONAL GRADES

BONNY LIGHT (NIGERIA)

Characteristics: Light and sweet crude oil, characterized by its low sulfur content and high API gravity.

Significance: Bonny Light is significant in the West African oil market, playing a crucial role in Nigeria's oil exports and regional pricing dynamics.

URALS (RUSSIA)

Characteristics: Medium sour crude oil, featuring a moderate API gravity and higher sulfur content compared to light sweet crudes.

Significance: Urals is essential for Russian oil exports, serving as a major blend in European and Asian markets, reflecting Russia's significant role in global energy markets.

MEXICAN BASKET (MEXICO)

Composition: A blend of Mexican crude oils, including heavy and medium grades.

Significance: Used as a regional benchmark in Mexico, the Mexican Basket influences domestic oil pricing and export strategies, reflecting Mexico's position in North American oil markets.

Understanding the diversity of crude oils beyond Brent and WTI is crucial for stakeholders in the global oil industry. Each crude grade possesses unique characteristics that influence its pricing, refining processes, and market dynamics.

From regional benchmarks like Dubai Crude and the OPEC Reference Basket to specific grades such as Bonny Light, Urals, and the Mexican Basket, these oils play integral roles in shaping regional and global oil markets, reflecting geopolitical, economic, and environmental factors impacting the energy sector.

PRICE DIFFERENTIALS AND ARBITRAGE OPPORTUNITIES

The differences in quality and location of crude oil lead to price differentials between various benchmarks. These differentials are influenced by factors such as transportation costs, refining capacity, and regional supply-demand dynamics.

Arbitrage Opportunities:

Traders can exploit price differentials through arbitrage strategies, buying cheaper crude in one market and selling it in another where prices are higher.

Arbitrage helps to balance supply and demand across different regions, contributing to market efficiency.

Understanding the different types of crude oil and their characteristics is essential for navigating the oil market. Brent Crude and WTI are the primary benchmarks, each with unique qualities and market significance.

PART 2: FUNDAMENTALS OF OIL TRADING

CHAPTER 4: SUPPLY AND DEMAND DYNAMICS

The oil market, like any other commodity market, is governed by the principles of supply and demand. Understanding these dynamics is crucial for traders, as they directly influence oil prices and market behavior. This chapter explores the key factors affecting supply and demand in the oil market and how they interact to shape price movements.

SUPPLY-SIDE FACTORS

The global oil market is intricately shaped by supply-side factors that range from geopolitical tensions and technological advancements to natural disasters and regulatory policies.

PRODUCTION LEVELS

Oil-Producing Countries:

Major Players: Countries like Saudi Arabia, Russia, and the United States wield significant control over global oil supply due to their large production capacities and reserves. Production decisions by these nations can have profound impacts on global oil prices and market stability.

OPEC: The Organization of the Petroleum Exporting Countries (OPEC) coordinates production levels among its member states to stabilize oil prices. OPEC sets production quotas to manage global oil supply, adjusting output in response to market conditions and geopolitical factors.

TECHNOLOGICAL ADVANCES

Extraction Technologies: Advances in extraction technologies, such as hydraulic fracturing (fracking) and deep-sea drilling, have revolutionized oil production. These technologies enable access to previously inaccessible reserves, particularly in regions like the United States, contributing to global supply growth.

Enhanced Oil Recovery (EOR): Techniques like carbon dioxide injection and thermal recovery enhance oil extraction rates from mature fields. EOR methods prolong the productive life of oil fields, maintaining or increasing production levels over time.

GEOPOLITICAL FACTORS

Political Stability: Political instability in major oil-producing regions, such as the Middle East or South America, can disrupt oil production. Shifts in government policies, sanctions, or civil unrest can lead to sudden production halts or output reductions.

Trade Policies: Tariffs, export restrictions, and trade agreements influence the movement of oil between countries. Changes in trade policies can affect the availability of oil in global markets, influencing supply dynamics.

NATURAL FACTORS

Weather Conditions: Severe weather events like hurricanes or typhoons can damage oil infrastructure and disrupt production operations. Climate patterns, such as El Niño or La Niña, can affect weather extremes, impacting oil supply routes and production schedules.

Natural Disasters: Earthquakes, floods, and other natural disasters pose immediate threats to oil infrastructure and operations. Rapid response measures are crucial to mitigating disruptions and restoring production capabilities swiftly.

DEMAND-SIDE FACTORS

Demand-side factors play a crucial role in shaping global oil markets, impacting consumption patterns and market dynamics. Economic growth, seasonal variations, technological advancements, and government policies collectively influence oil demand trends.

ECONOMIC GROWTH

Global Economic Health: The overall state of the global economy profoundly impacts oil demand. Economic expansion stimulates industrial production, increasing energy consumption and demand for oil.

Transportation: Growing economies lead to higher demand for transportation fuels, including gasoline and diesel.

Emerging Markets: Countries like China and India undergo rapid industrialization and urbanization, driving substantial increases in oil consumption. Infrastructure developments in emerging markets further bolster demand for oil in construction and transportation sectors.

SEASONAL VARIATIONS

Heating and Cooling Needs: Cold weather increases demand for heating oil, particularly in colder regions. Higher temperatures spur demand for gasoline as travel and leisure activities peak during summer months.

Holiday Travel: Holiday seasons, such as Thanksgiving and Christmas, witness spikes in travel activity, elevating demand for aviation fuel and gasoline.

TECHNOLOGICAL DEVELOPMENTS

Fuel Efficiency: Improvements in vehicle fuel efficiency and the rise of electric vehicles (EVs) reduce oil consumption growth rates. Adoption of renewable energy sources and EVs diminishes reliance on traditional oil-based fuels.

Industrial Innovation: Industrial processes incorporating cleaner technologies and alternative materials lessen reliance on oil-derived products, impacting demand dynamics.

GOVERNMENT POLICIES

Regulations and Subsidies: Stringent emissions regulations and carbon pricing encourage energy efficiency and renewable energy adoption, moderating oil demand growth. Government subsidies on fuel prices influence consumer behavior and overall fuel consumption patterns.

Strategic Reserves: Governments manage oil supply stability through strategic reserves, releasing or accumulating stocks in response to market disruptions or geopolitical tensions. Strategic reserve policies mitigate short-term demand fluctuations and ensure energy security during crises.

INTERPLAY BETWEEN SUPPLY AND DEMAND

The interplay between supply and demand forms the foundation of global oil market dynamics, dictating price movements and market stability. Equilibrium price levels are determined by the balance between oil production and consumption, with price elasticity influencing short-term demand responsiveness.

PRICE MECHANISM

Equilibrium Price: The balance between global oil supply and demand determines the equilibrium price. When demand surpasses supply, prices rise, incentivizing increased production and conservation efforts. Conversely, oversupply leads to price declines, prompting production cuts and higher consumption.

Market Stability: Fluctuations in supply and demand levels contribute to price volatility, influencing strategic decisions across the oil industry.

Price Elasticity: Oil exhibits relatively inelastic demand in the short term, meaning price changes do not immediately alter consumption levels. Over time, consumers and industries adjust behavior in response to sustained price shifts, impacting overall demand elasticity and market stability.

MARKET SENTIMENT AND SPECULATION

Trader Expectations: Market sentiment, driven by trader forecasts and expectations about future supply-demand balances, can significantly influence oil prices. Speculators engage in futures and options markets based on anticipated geopolitical events, economic indicators, and market sentiment, amplifying price volatility.

Hedging and Risk Management: Companies and investors utilize derivatives like futures, options, and swaps to hedge against price fluctuations. Hedging activities affect market dynamics by influencing future supply expectations and demand projections, contributing to price stability or volatility depending on market conditions

CASE STUDIES

The 2014-2016 Oil Glut

Cause: Advances in fracking technology led to a surge in U.S. oil production, contributing to an oversupply in the global market. At the same time, demand growth slowed due to economic conditions in key markets.

Effect: Oil prices plummeted from over $100 per barrel to around $30 per barrel, leading to financial strain on oil-producing countries and companies.

The 2020 Oil Price Crash

Cause: The COVID-19 pandemic led to a sharp decline in oil demand as global travel and economic activities were curtailed. Concurrently, a price war between Saudi Arabia and Russia initially increased supply.

Effect: Oil prices fell dramatically, with WTI futures briefly turning negative in April 2020 due to storage constraints and oversupply.

Understanding the dynamics of supply and demand is essential for navigating the oil market. Various factors, including production levels, technological advances, geopolitical events, economic growth, and seasonal variations, influence the supply and demand balance, thereby affecting oil prices. By comprehending these dynamics, traders can better anticipate market movements and develop informed trading strategies.

CHAPTER 5: KEY PLAYERS IN THE OIL MARKET

The oil market is a complex ecosystem comprising various entities that play significant roles in influencing oil supply, demand, and pricing. Understanding these key players—ranging from large multinational organizations to individual traders—is essential for anyone looking to trade oil or comprehend the market's intricacies.

This chapter provides an overview of the primary actors in the oil market: OPEC, non-OPEC oil producers, and speculators.

THE ORGANIZATION OF THE PETROLEUM EXPORTING COUNTRIES (OPEC)

OPEC was founded in 1960 by five oil-producing countries: Iran, Iraq, Kuwait, Saudi Arabia, and Venezuela. Its membership has since expanded to include 13 countries as of 2023.

OPEC's primary goal is to coordinate and unify petroleum policies among its member countries to ensure stable oil markets, secure fair and stable prices for petroleum producers, and provide a steady supply of oil to consuming nations.

OPEC Conference: The highest authority of OPEC, comprising delegations from member countries, meets biannually to set production quotas and policies. Member countries include Algeria, Angola, Congo, Equatorial Guinea, Gabon, Iran, Iraq, Kuwait, Libya, Nigeria, Saudi Arabia, United Arab Emirates and Venezuela

Quotas: OPEC sets production quotas for each member country to manage oil supply and influence global oil prices. These quotas aim to balance the market and avoid price volatility.

Price Influence: By adjusting production levels, OPEC can influence global oil prices. For example, reducing output can lead to higher prices, while increasing output can lower prices.

Market Stability: OPEC's efforts to stabilize the oil market help prevent extreme price fluctuations, benefiting both producers and consumers.

MAJOR NON-OPEC PRODUCERS

United States: The U.S. is one of the world's largest oil producers, thanks to advancements in hydraulic fracturing and shale oil extraction. The country produces significant quantities of both crude oil and natural gas liquids.

Russia: Russia is another leading non-OPEC oil producer with substantial reserves and production capacity. The country plays a critical role in the global oil market.

Canada: Canada has vast oil sands reserves, making it a significant oil producer. The country primarily exports its oil to the United States.

OPEC+: To enhance market stability, OPEC collaborates with non-OPEC oil-producing countries through the OPEC+ alliance. This broader coalition works together to coordinate production levels and manage global supply.

SPECULATORS AND FINANCIAL PLAYERS

Role of Speculators

Speculators are market participants who trade oil futures and other derivatives to profit from price fluctuations rather than physical delivery of the commodity. By buying and selling oil contracts, speculators add liquidity to the market and contribute to price discovery.

Types of Speculators

Hedge Funds: These institutional investors engage in oil trading to generate returns for their clients. They use sophisticated strategies to capitalize on market movements.

Retail Traders: Individual traders, often using online trading platforms, participate in oil markets by trading futures, options, and CFDs.

Proprietary Trading Firms: These firms trade oil contracts using their capital to profit from short-term price movements.

Impact on the Market

Volatility: Speculative trading can amplify price movements, leading to increased volatility. While this can create opportunities for traders, it can also pose risks.

Price Discovery: Speculators play a vital role in price discovery by responding to market information and events, helping to reflect the true value of oil in futures prices.

OTHER INFLUENTIAL ENTITIES

National Oil Companies (NOCs)

State-Owned Enterprises: Many countries have national oil companies, such as Saudi Aramco (Saudi Arabia), Gazprom (Russia), and Petrobras (Brazil), which control significant portions of the world's oil reserves and production.

Government Influence: NOCs often operate under government directives, balancing commercial objectives with national economic and political goals.

International Oil Companies (IOCs)

Major Corporations: IOCs, such as ExxonMobil, Chevron, BP, and Shell, are privately-owned companies that operate globally. They invest in exploration, production, refining, and marketing of oil and gas. IOCs drive technological innovation and make substantial investments in new oil and gas projects, influencing global supply.

Regulatory Bodies and Agencies

Market Oversight: Regulatory bodies, such as the Commodity Futures Trading Commission (CFTC) in the U.S., oversee trading practices and ensure market integrity. Agencies like the International Energy Agency (IEA) provide market analysis, policy recommendations, and forecasts that influence market perceptions and decisions.

The oil market is shaped by a diverse array of players, each contributing to the complex dynamics of supply, demand, and pricing. OPEC and its member countries aim to stabilize the market through coordinated production policies, while non-OPEC producers independently influence supply with their strategic decisions.

Speculators add liquidity and facilitate price discovery, though their activities can also increase volatility. Understanding the roles and interactions of these key players is crucial for anyone looking to trade oil or grasp the intricacies of the global oil market.

CHAPTER 6: IMPACT OF GEOPOLITICAL EVENTS

Geopolitical events significantly impact the oil market, often leading to price volatility and supply disruptions. Political stability, international conflicts, trade policies, and diplomatic relations are some of the key geopolitical factors that influence the global oil market. Understanding how these events affect oil prices and market dynamics is crucial for traders and investors.

POLITICAL STABILITY AND INSTABILITY

Oil-Producing Regions

Middle East: The Middle East is home to a significant portion of the world's oil reserves. Political instability in this region, such as conflicts in Iraq, Libya, and Syria, can disrupt oil production and export, leading to supply shortages and price spikes.

Africa: Countries like Nigeria and Angola are major oil producers. Political instability, militant activities, and civil unrest in these countries can impact oil production and supply.

Government Policies

Changes in government policies, such as the nationalization of oil industries, can affect production levels and investment in oil infrastructure. For example, Venezuela's nationalization of its oil industry led to a decline in production. New regulations, such as environmental policies and taxation, can influence oil production and pricing.

INTERNATIONAL CONFLICTS AND WARS

First Gulf War (1990-1991): The invasion of Kuwait by Iraq led to significant disruptions in oil supply, causing a sharp increase in oil prices. The subsequent military intervention by a coalition of countries restored stability, but the impact on oil prices was profound.

Second Gulf War (2003): The invasion of Iraq by the United States and its allies led to uncertainties in oil supply, contributing to price volatility.

Iran-Iraq War (1980-1988): The prolonged conflict between Iran and Iraq, both major oil producers, resulted in significant damage to their oil infrastructure and a reduction in oil exports, leading to higher oil prices.

Arab Spring (2010-2012): The wave of protests and uprisings across the Arab world affected several oil-producing countries, leading to supply disruptions and price fluctuations.

Russia-Ukraine War (2022-Present): The Russia-Ukraine War, starting in 2022, disrupted global oil markets by reducing Russian exports due to sanctions, causing supply shortages and higher prices. Supply chain disruptions from damaged pipelines and port blockages increased market volatility, leading to heightened speculative trading and fluctuating oil prices.

TRADE POLICIES AND SANCTIONS

Iran: Economic sanctions imposed by the United States and other countries on Iran have restricted its oil exports, affecting global supply and prices. The sanctions have led to reduced production and increased geopolitical tensions.

Venezuela: Economic sanctions on Venezuela have significantly impacted its oil industry, leading to a decline in production and export capabilities.

Russia: Economic sanctions on Russia due to the Ukraine conflict have severely affected its oil export capacity, influencing global oil prices and market dynamics.

US-China Trade War: The trade tensions between the United States and China have affected global economic growth and oil demand. Tariffs and trade restrictions can lead to uncertainties in the oil market, influencing prices.

OPEC AND PRODUCTION AGREEMENTS

OPEC Production Cuts: OPEC and its allies (OPEC+) often agree on production cuts to stabilize oil prices during periods of oversupply. These agreements can lead to significant changes in market dynamics and price levels. The effectiveness of OPEC's production cuts depends on member compliance. Non-compliance can undermine the efforts to stabilize prices.

Diplomatic Relations: The relationship between the United States and Saudi Arabia, a key OPEC member, has implications for global oil policies and market stability. Changes in diplomatic relations can influence production decisions and market perceptions.

STRATEGIC RESERVES AND EMERGENCY MEASURES

Strategic Petroleum Reserves (SPR): Countries maintain strategic petroleum reserves to mitigate the impact of supply disruptions. These reserves can be released during emergencies to stabilize markets and prevent price spikes. The United States, China, and Japan have significant strategic reserves that they can deploy in response to geopolitical events.

Coordinated Releases: In times of severe supply disruptions, countries may coordinate the release of strategic reserves to stabilize global oil markets. For example, the International Energy

Agency (IEA) coordinated the release of oil reserves during the 2011 Libyan crisis.

CASE STUDIES

The 1973 Oil Crisis: The Arab oil embargo, imposed by OPEC members in response to US support for Israel during the Yom Kippur War, led to a sharp reduction in oil supply. Oil prices quadrupled, leading to economic recessions in many countries and highlighting the vulnerability of global economies to oil supply disruptions.

The 2019 Attack on Saudi Oil Facilities: Drone attacks on Saudi Aramco's oil processing facilities at Abqaiq and Khurais significantly disrupted Saudi oil production. The attacks temporarily reduced Saudi oil output by about 50%, leading to a spike in oil prices and heightened concerns about the security of oil infrastructure.

Russia-Ukraine War (2022-Present): The invasion of Ukraine by Russia and the resulting geopolitical tensions. The conflict has led to widespread economic sanctions on Russia, disrupting its oil exports and leading to higher global oil prices. The uncertainty and volatility surrounding the war have contributed to significant price fluctuations in the oil market.

Geopolitical events have a profound impact on the oil market, influencing supply, demand, and prices. Political stability, international conflicts, trade policies, and strategic reserves are some of the key factors that traders must monitor to anticipate market movements and manage risk. By understanding the interplay between geopolitics and the oil market, traders can make informed decisions and develop effective strategies to navigate this volatile market.

PART 3: OIL MARKET INSTRUMENTS

CHAPTER 7: UNDERSTANDING OIL CFDS

Contracts for Difference (CFDs) are financial derivatives that allow traders to speculate on the price movements of oil without owning the underlying asset. CFDs let traders guess if the price of oil will go up or down. Instead of buying actual oil, they make a deal with a broker.

When they close the deal, they get money based on how much the oil's price changed from when they started the deal to when they ended it. It's like betting on whether the price of something will go up or down, without actually owning it.

CHARACTERISTICS OF CFDS

CFDs offer unique characteristics that appeal to traders looking for leveraged opportunities, flexibility in market positioning, and the simplicity of not dealing with physical commodities.

Leverage: CFDs allow traders to control a large position in oil with a relatively small initial investment, known as margin. This leverage can significantly amplify potential profits, as gains are calculated based on the full value of the position. However, leverage also increases the risk of larger losses, as any adverse price movement affects the entire position size.

Flexibility: Traders can "go long" (buy) CFDs if they expect oil prices to rise. This means they will profit if the price of oil increases. Conversely, traders can "go short" (sell) CFDs if they anticipate a decline in oil prices. This allows them to profit from falling prices. This flexibility to trade in both directions enables traders to adapt to different market conditions and take advantage of various price movements.

NO OWNERSHIP

Unlike traditional oil trading, where physical delivery and storage of oil might be required, CFD trading involves no ownership of the actual oil commodity. This eliminates the complexities and costs associated with storing and handling physical oil, making it easier for traders to participate in the oil market. CFD trading is purely speculative, focusing on price movements rather than the logistics of buying and storing the physical asset.

HOW OIL CFDS WORK

Trading oil through Contracts for Difference (CFDs) offers investors and traders a flexible and leveraged approach to participate in oil price movements without owning the underlying asset.

CONTRACT SPECIFICATIONS

Volume and Size: Each oil CFD contract specifies a fixed volume of oil, typically measured in barrels (e.g., 1,000 barrels per contract).

Margin Requirements: Traders are required to maintain a margin deposit to open and hold positions, which varies based on the broker and market conditions.

Trading Conditions: Brokers set specific conditions for trading oil CFDs, including leverage options, commission fees, and other terms that traders must adhere to.

PRICE QUOTATION

Market Pricing: Oil CFD prices directly correlate with the underlying market prices of crude oil futures contracts. Prices are adjusted for factors such as broker fees, spreads, and market liquidity, ensuring alignment with prevailing market conditions.

EXPIRY AND ROLLOVER

Expiry Dates: Oil CFD contracts have predefined expiry dates, typically corresponding to the expiration dates of the underlying futures contracts.

Rollover Process: Prior to expiry, traders may choose to roll over their positions to the next contract period to avoid settlement and maintain exposure.

Considerations: Traders should be aware of rollover costs, which may include adjustments in contract pricing due to market conditions and broker fees.

MARGIN TRADING

Margin trading with CFDs provides traders with the opportunity to control large positions with a small initial investment through the use of leverage. While this can lead to significant profits, it also increases the risk of substantial losses. Understanding margin requirements and leverage ratios is essential for successful and prudent trading in the CFD market.

MARGIN REQUIREMENTS

Initial Deposit: To open a CFD position, traders must deposit a portion of the total trade value with their broker. This initial deposit is known as the margin.

Example: If the margin requirement is 10%, and a trader wants to control a position worth $10,000 in oil CFDs, they only need to deposit $1,000 as margin.

Increased Buying Power: This requirement allows traders to control much larger positions with a relatively small amount of upfront capital, enhancing their buying power in the market.

LEVERAGE RATIO

The leverage ratio determines how much larger a position a trader can control compared to their margin deposit. For example, a leverage ratio of 10:1 means that for every $1 of margin, a trader can control $10 worth of the underlying asset.

Variable Ratios: Leverage ratios can vary depending on the broker and the regulatory environment. Common leverage ratios range from 5:1 to 30:1 or higher.

Example: With a leverage ratio of 10:1, a trader with a $1,000 margin can control a $10,000 position in oil CFDs.

Potential Gains and Losses: Leverage can significantly amplify potential profits. A 1% increase in the price of oil on a $10,000 position results in a $100 profit, which is a 10% return on the $1,000 margin. However, leverage also increases the potential for losses. A 1% decrease in the price of oil on the same $10,000 position results in a $100 loss, which is a 10% loss on the margin.

Risk Management: Effective risk management strategies, such as setting stop-loss orders and careful position sizing, are crucial to mitigating the risks associated with leveraged trading.

ADVANTAGES OF OIL CFD TRADING

Speculative Opportunities: Traders can profit from both rising (going long) and falling (going short) oil prices, depending on their market analysis and strategy. CFDs typically offer high liquidity, allowing traders to enter and exit positions quickly without significant price slippage. CFDs provide access to global oil markets and various oil benchmarks (e.g., Brent, WTI) with ease, regardless of geographical location.

Cost Efficiency: Unlike physical oil trading, CFD trading does not involve storage costs, insurance, or transportation fees associated with owning the commodity. CFDs generally involve lower transaction costs compared to traditional commodity trading, making them cost-effective for frequent trading.

RISKS OF OIL CFD TRADING

Leverage Risks: Leverage amplifies both potential profits and losses. Traders can lose more than their initial investment if the market moves against their position. If a trade moves against the trader, they may be required to deposit additional funds (**margin call**) to maintain the position, potentially leading to further losses or position closure.

Market Volatility: Oil prices can be highly volatile, influenced by geopolitical events, economic data releases, and supply-demand dynamics. This volatility can lead to rapid price movements and increased trading risks.

Counterparty Risk: CFD trading involves trading with a broker as the counterparty. Traders are exposed to the credit risk of the broker, including the risk of default or insolvency.

Oil CFDs offer traders a flexible and accessible way to participate in the global oil market, allowing them to profit from both rising and falling prices without owning the physical commodity.

While CFDs provide advantages such as leverage, liquidity, and cost-efficiency, they also entail risks including leverage risks, market volatility, and counterparty risks. Traders should carefully assess their risk tolerance, employ risk management strategies, and conduct thorough market analysis when engaging in oil CFD trading.

CHAPTER 8: INTRODUCTION TO OIL FUTURES

Oil futures contracts are standardized agreements to buy or sell a specified quantity of oil (typically crude oil) at a predetermined price on a future delivery date. They are traded on futures exchanges and serve as a key instrument for hedging and speculation in the oil market.

Futures contracts specify the quality, quantity (e.g., barrels), delivery location, and delivery date of the oil. This standardization facilitates trading and price transparency. Each futures contract has a specific expiration date, after which the contract must be settled by physical delivery or cash settlement. Oil futures markets are highly liquid, allowing for efficient price discovery and ease of entry and exit for traders.

TYPES OF OIL FUTURES CONTRACTS

Understanding the different types of oil futures contracts, their sources, exchanges, and significance helps traders and investors navigate the complexities of oil trading and make informed decisions based on market conditions and geopolitical factors.

1. WEST TEXAS INTERMEDIATE (WTI) CRUDE OIL FUTURES

Location: WTI crude oil is sourced from the United States, primarily from Texas and surrounding states.

Exchange: These futures are traded on the New York Mercantile Exchange (NYMEX).

Symbol: CL

Contract Size: 1,000 barrels of crude oil.

Benchmark Status: WTI is a key benchmark for oil prices in North America and is one of the most actively traded oil futures contracts globally.

Price Determination: The contract's price is influenced by U.S. production levels, storage capacities, and geopolitical factors affecting North American supply.

2. BRENT CRUDE OIL FUTURES

Location: Brent crude oil is sourced from the North Sea.

Exchange: These futures are traded on the Intercontinental Exchange (ICE).

Symbol: BZ

Contract Size: 1,000 barrels of crude oil.

Global Benchmark: Brent is the most widely used benchmark for oil prices globally, affecting oil pricing in Europe, Africa, and the Middle East.

Price Determination: The contract's price is influenced by global supply and demand dynamics, geopolitical events

3. DUBAI CRUDE OIL FUTURES

Location: Dubai crude oil is sourced from the Persian Gulf.

Exchange: These futures are traded on the Dubai Mercantile Exchange (DME).

Symbol: Oman Crude Oil Futures (DME Oman) is often used as a proxy for Dubai crude.

Contract Size: 1,000 barrels of crude oil.

Regional Benchmark: Dubai crude serves as a pricing benchmark for oil produced in the Middle East and is commonly used for pricing Persian Gulf exports to Asia.

Price Determination: The contract's price is influenced by regional supply and demand, Middle Eastern

4. OPEC BASKET CRUDE OIL FUTURES

Composition: The OPEC Basket is a weighted average of oil prices from various OPEC member countries.

Exchange: Futures based on the OPEC Basket are less common but can be traded on specific exchanges or over-the-counter (OTC) markets.

Symbol: Varies depending on the specific exchange or OTC agreement.

Contract Size: Typically 1,000 barrels of crude oil.

OPEC Influence: The OPEC Basket provides a comprehensive benchmark for the collective output of OPEC member countries.

Price Determination: The contract's price is influenced by OPEC production quotas, member compliance, and global supply and demand.

5. OTHER REGIONAL CRUDE OIL FUTURES

BONNY LIGHT (NIGERIA):

Location: Sourced from Nigeria.

Significance: Important for West African oil markets and used as a benchmark for regional pricing.

URALS (RUSSIA):

Location: Sourced from Russia.

Significance: Medium sour crude, crucial for Russian oil exports and European markets.

MEXICAN BASKET (MEXICO):

Location: A blend of Mexican crudes.

Significance: Used as a regional benchmark for Mexican oil exports.

HOW OIL FUTURES TRADING WORKS

Trading Mechanics: Futures contracts are traded on regulated exchanges, with participants including hedgers (e.g., producers, consumers) and speculators (e.g., institutional investors, individual traders). Traders can take long positions (buy futures) if they anticipate rising oil prices or short positions (sell futures) if they expect prices to fall.

Margin Requirements: Traders are required to deposit an initial margin with the exchange to open a futures position. This margin serves as collateral and ensures performance on the contract. Futures positions are marked-to-market daily, with traders required to maintain a minimum margin level. Margin calls may occur if the account falls below this level.

HEDGING WITH OIL FUTURES

Hedging with oil futures is a critical strategy for managing the financial risks associated with oil price volatility. Producers and consumers of oil use these contracts to stabilize their costs and revenues, while speculators contribute to market liquidity and price efficiency.

PURPOSE OF HEDGING

Risk Management: Oil producers, such as drilling companies, and consumers, such as airlines, use oil futures to hedge against the risk of price fluctuations. By locking in prices through futures contracts, they can stabilize their costs and revenues.

Example: An oil producer expecting to sell oil in the future can sell oil futures contracts now to lock in a favorable price. If oil prices fall, the loss in the spot market is offset by the gain in the futures market.

This strategy helps in reducing the uncertainty and financial risks associated with the highly volatile oil market, ensuring more predictable financial planning and budgeting.

Speculation: Unlike hedgers, speculators aim to profit from price changes in the oil market. They buy or sell futures contracts based on their expectations of future price movements. Speculators add liquidity to the market, making it easier for hedgers to enter and exit positions. Their activity also contributes to more efficient price discovery and market stability.

Example: A trader who anticipates an increase in oil prices might buy oil futures contracts. If the price rises as expected, they can sell the contracts at a higher price, making a profit.

SETTLEMENT METHODS

1. PHYSICAL DELIVERY:

If an oil futures contract is held until its expiration date, the seller is obligated to deliver the physical oil, and the buyer is required to take possession of it. The delivery occurs at a specified location, known as the delivery point. The delivery process follows standardized procedures to ensure the quality and quantity of the oil meet the contract specifications.

Parties involved in physical delivery must manage the logistics of transporting the oil to the delivery point. This includes arranging for trucks, pipelines, or ships to move the oil.

Buyers must arrange for storage facilities to hold the oil. Storage costs can include renting storage tanks or leasing space in oil storage facilities. Both parties must ensure the oil meets quality standards as specified in the contract, which may involve testing and certification processes.

2. CASH SETTLEMENT:

Many futures contracts are settled financially, meaning no physical delivery of oil takes place. Instead, the contract is settled based on the price difference between the contract price and the market price at expiration. At the contract's expiration, the net difference between the agreed-upon futures price and the spot price is settled in cash. If the futures price is higher, the seller pays the buyer the difference, and vice versa.

Cash settlement is often based on a specified index or price assessment, which reflects the market price of oil at the time of contract expiration. Using market-based pricing ensures transparency and fairness in the settlement process, as the prices are determined by widely recognized and accepted market assessments.

ADVANTAGES OF OIL FUTURES TRADING

Price Discovery: Futures markets provide transparent and real-time price information, reflecting supply-demand fundamentals and market sentiment. Traders can capitalize on price discrepancies between futures and spot markets through arbitrage strategies.

Risk Management: Futures contracts enable effective hedging against oil price volatility, allowing producers, consumers, and traders to manage price risks. Institutional investors and funds use oil futures to diversify portfolios and manage overall investment risk.

RISKS OF OIL FUTURES TRADING

Market Volatility: Oil futures prices can be volatile, influenced by geopolitical events, economic data releases, and supply-demand dynamics. This volatility can lead to rapid price movements and increased trading risks. Futures trading involves leverage, amplifying potential gains and losses. Margin calls may occur if market movements deplete account balances.

Counterparty and Operational Risks: Futures trading involves counterparty risk, though exchanges typically manage this risk through clearinghouses and margin requirements. Traders must navigate operational risks, including execution errors, technological failures, and regulatory changes affecting trading conditions.

Oil futures contracts play a vital role in the global oil market, providing essential tools for price discovery, risk management, and speculation. These standardized contracts allow participants to hedge against oil price fluctuations, facilitating stability for producers, consumers, and investors.

While futures trading offers advantages such as liquidity, transparency, and effective risk management, it also entails risks including market volatility, leverage, and operational challenges. Traders and investors should conduct thorough analysis, implement risk management strategies, and stay informed about market developments when engaging in oil futures trading.

CHAPTER 9: BASICS OF OIL OPTIONS

Oil options provide the buyer (holder) with the right, but not the obligation, to buy (call option) or sell (put option) a specified quantity of oil at a predetermined price (strike price) on or before the expiration date. Options are derivative contracts traded on exchanges, offering flexibility for hedging and speculation in the oil market.

KEY TERMS

Understanding the key terms and types of oil options is essential for effectively navigating the options market.

Call Option: A financial contract that gives the holder the right, but not the obligation, to buy a specified amount of oil at a predetermined price (the strike price) within a certain period.

Traders use call options when they anticipate an increase in oil prices. If the market price rises above the strike price, the option holder can buy the oil at the lower strike price and potentially sell it at the market price for a profit.

Put Option: A financial contract that gives the holder the right, but not the obligation, to sell a specified amount of oil at a predetermined price (the strike price) within a certain period.

Traders use put options when they expect a decrease in oil prices. If the market price falls below the strike price, the option holder can sell the oil at the higher strike price and potentially buy it back at the lower market price.

Premium: The price paid by the option buyer to the option seller (writer) for the rights granted by the option contract. The premium is influenced by various factors, including the current price of oil, the strike price, the time remaining until expiration, and the volatility of the oil market.

TYPES OF OIL OPTIONS

European vs. American Options:

European Options: These options can only be exercised on the expiration date itself. Suitable for traders with a specific outlook on the price movement by the expiration date, offering simplicity and generally lower premiums compared to American options.

American Options: These options can be exercised at any time before or on the expiration date. Provides greater flexibility for traders, allowing them to capitalize on favorable price movements at any point during the option's life.

OPTION STYLES

Vanilla Options: Standardized options contracts with straightforward terms, typically including only call and put options. Easy to understand and widely used in the market, suitable for most trading and hedging strategies.

Exotic Options: Customized options with more complex features tailored to specific trading needs. Types of exotic options:

Barrier Options: These options become active or inactive if the underlying asset reaches a predetermined price level.

Asian Options: The payoff depends on the average price of the underlying asset over a specified period, rather than the price at expiration.

Usage: Exotic options are used by traders seeking to hedge specific risks or to implement sophisticated trading strategies that are not possible with vanilla options.

HOW OIL OPTIONS TRADING WORKS

Understanding how oil options trading works involves grasping the key factors that influence option premiums and employing various trading strategies.

OPTION PREMIUM

Factors Affecting Premium:

Underlying Oil Price: The current price of oil significantly impacts the option premium. For call options, a higher underlying price increases the premium, while for put options, it decreases the premium.

Volatility: Higher market volatility generally increases option premiums. Volatility reflects the market's uncertainty about future oil price movements, making options more valuable as hedging tools.

Time to Expiration: The longer the time until an option's expiration, the higher the premium. This is because there is more time for the underlying oil price to move favorably.

Interest Rates: Changes in interest rates can affect option premiums. Higher interest rates typically increase call option premiums and decrease put option premiums due to the cost-of-carry model.

Option Pricing Models:

Black-Scholes Model: This model uses mathematical formulas to calculate the fair price of European options. It considers factors such as the current price of the underlying asset, the option's strike price, time to expiration, risk-free interest rate, and volatility.

Binomial Model: This model creates a binomial tree to evaluate American options, which can be exercised at any time before expiration. It breaks down the time to expiration into discrete intervals and calculates the potential outcomes at each step, providing a more flexible and accurate pricing method for options with early exercise features.

OPTION STRATEGIES

Buying Calls and Puts:

Call Options: Traders buy call options when they expect the price of oil to rise. Owning a call option gives them the right to purchase oil at the strike price, potentially below market value if prices increase.

Example: If a trader buys a call option with a strike price of $70 per barrel and the market price rises to $80, they can exercise the option to buy oil at $70 and sell it at the market price for a profit.

Put Options: Traders buy put options when they anticipate a decline in oil prices. Owning a put option gives them the right to sell oil at the strike price, potentially above market value if prices drop.

Example: If a trader buys a put option with a strike price of $70 per barrel and the market price falls to $60, they can exercise the option to sell oil at $70 and buy it at the market price for a profit.

Selling Calls and Puts:

Call Options: Option sellers (writers) sell call options to collect premiums, expecting the price of oil to remain below the strike price. If the option is not exercised, the seller keeps the premium. If the market price rises above the strike price, the seller is obligated to sell oil at the lower strike price, potentially incurring a loss.

Example: A trader sells a call option with a strike price of $70 and collects a premium of $5. If the market price stays below $70, the option expires worthless, and the seller keeps the premium.

Put Options: Option sellers sell put options to collect premiums, expecting the price of oil to stay above the strike price. If the option is not exercised, the seller retains the premium. If the market price falls below the strike price, the seller is obligated to buy oil at the higher strike price, potentially incurring a loss.

Example: A trader sells a put option with a strike price of $70 and collects a premium of $5. If the market price stays above $70, the option expires worthless, and the seller keeps the premium.

ADVANTAGES OF OIL OPTIONS TRADING

Limited Risk, Unlimited Potential: Option buyers' risk is limited to the premium paid, providing downside protection compared to futures or CFDs. Option buyers can potentially profit from significant price movements in the underlying oil market.

Flexibility and Strategic Use: Options offer flexibility for hedging against adverse price movements, allowing producers and consumers to manage price risks effectively. Traders can use options to speculate on short-term price movements or volatility in the oil market, leveraging different trading strategies.

RISKS OF OIL OPTIONS TRADING

Time Decay: Options lose value over time (time decay), particularly affecting out-of-the-money options as expiration approaches. Time decay accelerates as expiration nears, impacting option premiums and potential profitability.

Volatility and Market Risk: High volatility can increase option premiums but also amplifies trading risks and potential losses. Rapid changes in oil prices and unexpected market events can affect option values and trading outcomes.

PRACTICAL CONSIDERATIONS

Option Expiration and Exercise: Option holders may choose to exercise options to realize profits or manage risks, depending on market conditions and trading objectives. Options may be automatically exercised if they are in-the-money at expiration, leading to delivery or cash settlement.

Option Strategies: Popular option strategies include buying calls or puts, selling covered calls, and employing spreads (e.g., bull spreads, bear spreads) to manage risk and enhance profitability. Traders should implement risk management techniques, such as setting stop-loss orders and diversifying strategies, to mitigate potential losses.

Oil options provide traders and investors with versatile tools for managing risk, speculating on price movements, and enhancing portfolio strategies in the dynamic oil market. Options offer advantages such as limited risk, strategic flexibility, and potential for significant profits, but they also involve risks including time decay, volatility exposure, and market fluctuations.

Traders should carefully assess market conditions, employ effective trading strategies, and utilize risk management techniques when engaging in oil options trading. By understanding the fundamentals, types, strategies, and risks associated with oil options, participants can navigate this complex market with confidence and capitalize on opportunities effectively.

PART 4: MARKET ANALYSIS TECHNIQUES

CHAPTER 10: FUNDAMENTAL ANALYSIS FOR OIL TRADING

Fundamental analysis involves evaluating the intrinsic value of an asset by analyzing economic, financial, and other qualitative and quantitative factors that could influence its price in the future. For oil trading, fundamental analysis focuses on understanding supply-demand dynamics, geopolitical events, economic indicators, and other factors impacting oil prices.

KEY FACTORS IN FUNDAMENTAL ANALYSIS FOR OIL TRADING

Integrating fundamental analysis into oil trading strategies can enhance both long-term investment and short-term trading success. You need to observe the trend – if it is going up or down.

1. SUPPLY FACTORS

Production Levels: Closely monitor oil production from key producers, including OPEC, Russia, the United States, and other significant non-OPEC countries. Fluctuations in production levels can signal changes in supply, impacting oil prices. Regularly analyze production quotas set by OPEC, as their collective decisions can lead to significant adjustments in global oil supply.

Inventories: Assess oil inventories in major storage facilities, including those in the United States (like Cushing, Oklahoma), to understand current supply levels. Evaluate the status of strategic reserves (Strategic Petroleum Reserves - SPR) maintained by governments, which can be tapped to manage supply and demand imbalances.

Exploration and Production Trends: Analyze innovations in oil exploration and extraction technologies, such as hydraulic fracturing (fracking) and deep-sea drilling, which can increase production efficiency and access to new reserves. Track the number of active drilling rigs and new oilfield discoveries to gauge future production capabilities.

2. DEMAND FACTORS

Economic Growth: Monitor key economic indicators like GDP growth rates, industrial production, and consumer spending, which directly influence oil consumption patterns. Pay particular attention to rapidly industrializing regions such as China and India, where economic expansion can significantly increase oil demand.

Transportation and Industrial Activity: Track trends in transportation (automotive, aviation, and shipping), manufacturing, and construction, which are major oil consumers. Observe investments in infrastructure projects that could boost oil demand.

Seasonal Demand Variations: Consider increased demand for heating oil during winter in colder regions and the rise in gasoline consumption during summer vacation periods in many parts of the world.

3. GEOPOLITICAL AND ENVIRONMENTAL FACTORS

Geopolitical Events: Assess the impact of geopolitical tensions, conflicts, and sanctions in oil-producing regions, which can disrupt supply routes and production. Evaluate trade policies and disputes that may affect oil imports and exports.

Environmental Policies: Analyze environmental regulations and policies, including international agreements like the Paris Agreement, aimed at reducing carbon emissions and potentially impacting oil consumption. Consider the implications of carbon pricing mechanisms, such as carbon taxes and cap-and-trade systems, on oil demand.

4. CURRENCY AND MONETARY POLICY

Currency Exchange Rates: Since oil is globally priced in US dollars, exchange rate fluctuations play a significant role. A stronger dollar can make oil more expensive for holders of other currencies, potentially reducing demand. Evaluating the impact of currency volatility on the economies of oil-importing and exporting countries, as well as their oil trade balances, is crucial.

Monetary Policy: Monitoring central bank decisions, such as interest rate changes and quantitative easing measures, is important as they influence economic stability and oil market dynamics. Assessing inflation trends is also key, as higher inflation can erode purchasing power and affect oil demand.

ANALYTICAL TOOLS AND DATA SOURCES

1. ECONOMIC REPORTS AND DATA RELEASES

EIA Reports: Utilizing data from the U.S. Energy Information Administration (EIA), including weekly petroleum status reports, crude oil inventory data, and international energy outlooks.

IEA Reports: Reviewing publications and forecasts from the International Energy Agency (IEA) on global energy trends, supply-demand balances, and policy developments.

2. MARKET SENTIMENT AND SPECULATIVE ACTIVITY

Commitment of Traders (COT) Report: Analyzing positions held by commercial hedgers, large speculators, and small traders to gauge market sentiment and potential price trends.

Speculative Trading Activity: Monitoring futures and options trading volumes, open interest, and price movements driven by speculative activities.

3. GEOPOLITICAL NEWS AND EVENTS

News Outlets: Following geopolitical news from reputable sources covering developments in oil-producing regions, diplomatic relations, sanctions, and conflicts impacting global oil markets.

Event Calendar: Staying informed about scheduled events, OPEC meetings, economic summits, and policy announcements influencing oil price volatility.

USING FUNDAMENTAL ANALYSIS IN OIL TRADING STRATEGIES

1. LONG-TERM INVESTMENT STRATEGIES

Value Investing: Investors seek out oil companies or assets undervalued based on fundamental analysis. This involves evaluating factors such as production costs, reserve quality, and potential for long-term demand growth. Analyzing companies with lower production costs helps identify those better positioned to withstand market downturns and remain profitable.

Additionally, assessing the quality and quantity of an oil company's reserves, including proven and probable reserves, provides insight into its long-term production potential. Evaluating long-term demand projections, considering factors like global economic growth, industrialization in emerging markets, and shifts in energy consumption patterns, is also crucial.

Dividend Yield Analysis: Investors focus on oil companies that consistently offer stable dividend yields, signaling financial health and a commitment to returning value to shareholders. Analyzing payout ratios ensures dividends are sustainable without jeopardizing the company's financial stability.

A lower payout ratio can provide a buffer for maintaining dividends during market downturns. Additionally, reviewing key financial metrics such as cash flow, debt levels, and profitability helps assess the overall financial health and stability of the company.

2. SHORT-TERM TRADING STRATEGIES

News Trading: Reacting swiftly to market-moving news and data releases that impact oil prices, such as geopolitical events, production reports, and economic indicators. Employ rapid execution strategies to enter and exit positions based on immediate market reactions. This requires access to real-time data and efficient trading platforms. Implement robust risk management techniques, such as stop-loss orders, to protect against adverse price movements resulting from volatile news events.

Event-Based Trading: Capitalize on anticipated price volatility around scheduled events like OPEC meetings, economic reports, and policy announcements. Trading strategies may include positioning trades ahead of or reacting to outcomes of OPEC meetings where production quotas and policies are decided.

Monitor economic indicators such as GDP growth, employment data, and industrial production reports that can influence oil demand projections. Strategically position trades to benefit from expected market movements surrounding these events, using fundamental analysis to anticipate likely outcomes.

Fundamental analysis plays a crucial role in oil trading, providing traders and investors with valuable insights into the underlying factors driving supply, demand, and price dynamics in the global oil market. By understanding and analyzing economic indicators, geopolitical events, environmental policies, and other fundamental factors, participants can make informed decisions and develop effective trading strategies.

However, fundamental analysis is complemented by technical analysis and risk management techniques to navigate the complexities and uncertainties of the oil market effectively.

CHAPTER 11: TECHNICAL ANALYSIS: CHARTS AND INDICATORS

Technical analysis involves studying historical price and volume data to identify trends, patterns, and market behavior in order to predict future price movements. For oil trading, technical analysis utilizes charts and technical indicators to make informed trading decisions based on market trends and patterns.

TYPES OF CHARTS IN TECHNICAL ANALYSIS

1. CANDLESTICK CHARTS

Candlestick charts: moneysukh.com

Candlestick charts are a powerful tool in technical analysis, illustrating price movements over a specified time period (e.g., day, week, hour). Each candlestick represents one time period and displays four key pieces of information: the opening price, closing price, highest price, and lowest price.

The body of the candlestick shows the range between the opening and closing prices. The lines (wicks or shadows) extending from the body indicate the high and low prices.

PATTERNS:

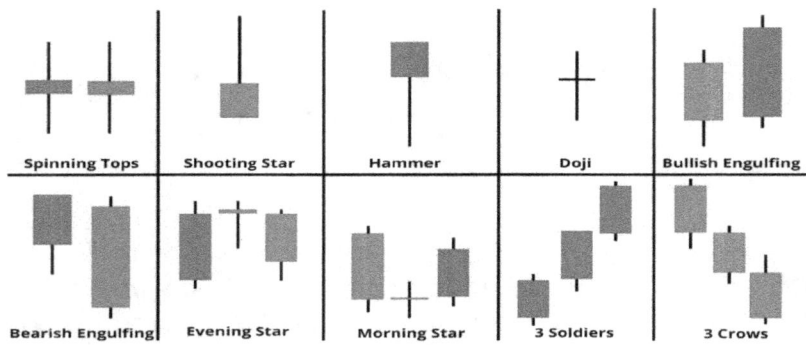

Candlestick patterns: medium.com

Doji: A candlestick where the opening and closing prices are very close or equal, indicating indecision in the market and potential reversal points.

Hammer: A candlestick with a small body and a long lower wick, suggesting a potential bullish reversal after a downtrend.

Engulfing: A pattern where a small candlestick is followed by a larger candlestick that completely engulfs the previous one, indicating a potential reversal in market direction.

Morning Star and Evening Star: Patterns that signify potential reversal points, with the morning star indicating a bullish reversal and the evening star indicating a bearish reversal.

2. LINE CHARTS

Line charts plot only the closing prices over time, connecting them with a continuous line. This simplicity makes them easy to understand and useful for identifying overall price trends.

Line charts are effective for visualizing long-term trends and comparing historical price movements, making it easier to identify key support and resistance levels.

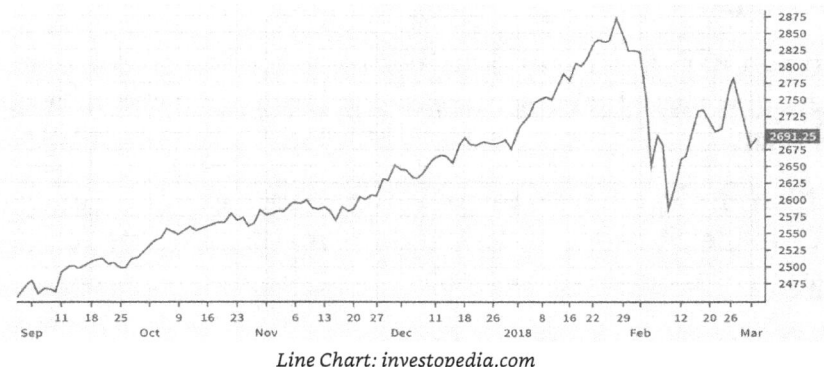

Line Chart: investopedia.com

It is best used when the focus is on the closing price, which many traders consider the most important price of the day.

3. BAR CHARTS

Bar Chart: forextraininggroup.com

Bar charts provide a more detailed view of price movements within a given time period compared to line charts. Each bar represents one time period and includes the opening price (a horizontal tick on the left), closing price (a horizontal tick on the right), high price (top of the bar), and low price (bottom of the bar).

Bar charts are useful for analyzing price volatility and market sentiment, as the length of the bars can indicate the degree of price movement within each period.

BAR CHART PATTERNS:

Inside Bar: A bar with a lower high and higher low compared to the previous bar, indicating consolidation and potential breakout points.

Outside Bar: A bar with a higher high and lower low than the previous bar, suggesting increased volatility and potential trend reversals.

Bullish and Bearish Patterns: Patterns such as bullish and bearish bars help traders understand the market sentiment and potential future price movements.

KEY TECHNICAL INDICATORS FOR OIL TRADING

1. MOVING AVERAGES

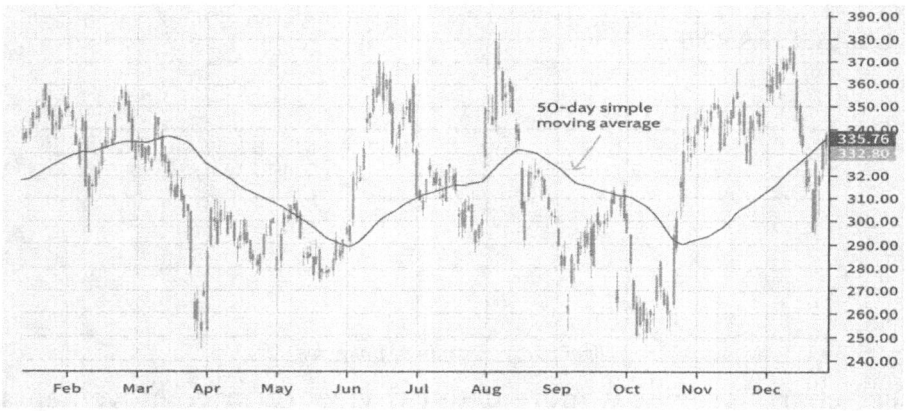

Simple Moving Average (SMA): investopedia.com

Simple moving averages (SMA) calculate the average price over a specified period, while exponential moving averages (EMA) give more weight to recent prices. They help identify trend direction and generate buy/sell signals.

Simple Moving Average (SMA) and Exponential Moving Average (EMA) are commonly used to smooth out price data and identify trend direction (e.g., 50-day SMA, 200-day SMA). Traders use moving average crossovers (e.g., 50-day crossing above 200-day) to signal potential buy or sell opportunities.

2. RELATIVE STRENGTH INDEX (RSI)

Relative Strength Index (RSI) bottom chart. commodity.com

A momentum oscillator measuring the speed and change of price movements on a scale from 0 to 100. An RSI above 70 indicates overbought conditions, suggesting a potential price correction, while an RSI below 30 indicates oversold conditions, suggesting a potential price rise. RSI divergence with price movements can signal potential reversals or continuation patterns.

3. BOLLINGER BANDS

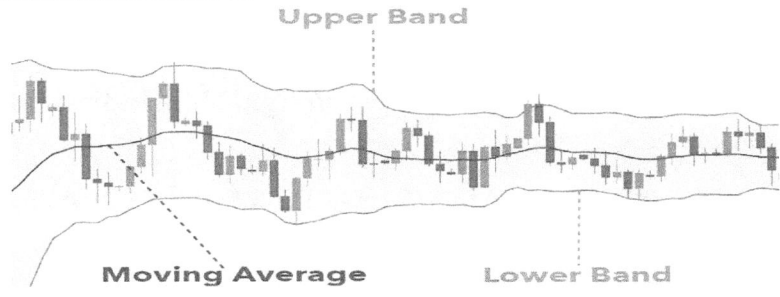

Bollinger Bands : dailyfx.com

Bollinger Bands consist of a simple moving average (SMA) with upper and lower bands based on standard deviations of price volatility. The bands expand and contract based on volatility, helping traders identify overbought or oversold conditions and potential price breakouts. When the bands widen, it indicates increased volatility, and when they narrow, it indicates decreased volatility. This helps traders anticipate potential price movements and make informed trading decisions.

4. MACD (Moving Average Convergence Divergence)

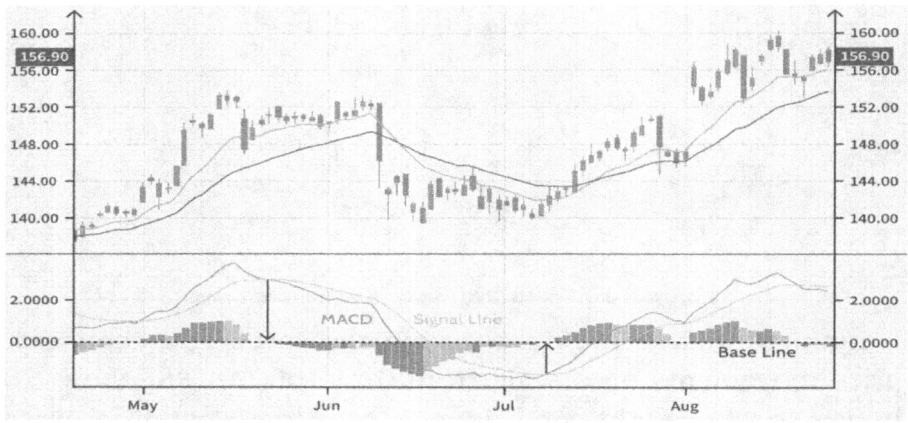

Moving Average Convergence Divergence (MACD): investopedia.com

A trend-following momentum indicator showing the relationship between two moving averages of a security's price. The MACD line is the difference between the 26-period EMA and the 12-period EMA, with a 9-period EMA signal line plotted on top. The MACD histogram plots the difference between the MACD line and the signal line, helping identify trend strength.

MACD line crosses above or below the signal line indicate potential buy or sell signals.

USING TECHNICAL ANALYSIS IN OIL TRADING STRATEGIES

1. TREND IDENTIFICATION

Identifying the main direction in which the oil market is moving over a longer period is crucial for making informed trading decisions. Trends can be categorized as follows:

CHAPTER 11: TECHNICAL ANALYSIS: CHARTS AND INDICATORS | 61

Trend Trading: danielsash.medium.com

Uptrend: Characterized by higher highs and higher lows. Traders look for opportunities to buy (go long) during uptrends, as the general direction of the market is upward.

Downtrend: Characterized by lower highs and lower lows. Traders look for opportunities to sell (go short) during downtrends, as the general direction of the market is downward.

Sideways Trend: The market moves within a range with no clear upward or downward direction. Traders may use range-bound strategies, buying at support levels and selling at resistance levels within the established range.

2. SUPPORT AND RESISTANCE LEVELS

Support and resistance: dailyfx.com

Support Levels: These are price levels where a downward trend tends to pause due to a concentration of buying interest. Traders look for buying opportunities near support levels, anticipating that the price will bounce back up.

Resistance Levels: These are price levels where an upward trend tends to pause due to a concentration of selling interest. Traders look for selling opportunities near resistance levels, expecting that the price will fall back down.

Identifying Support and Resistance:

Historical Price Data: Reviewing past price movements to identify recurring levels where prices have previously reversed direction.

Psychological Levels: Round numbers (e.g., $50, $100) often act as strong support or resistance levels due to their psychological impact on traders.

Indicators: Using tools like Bollinger Bands, RSI, and moving averages to confirm support and resistance levels.

3. CHART PATTERNS

A. Reversal Patterns:

A reversal pattern indicates that the current trend is likely to change direction.

Head and Shoulders: A pattern with three peaks, where the middle peak (head) is higher than the two side peaks (shoulders). It indicates a potential reversal from an uptrend to a downtrend.

Double Tops and Bottoms: Two consecutive peaks (tops) or troughs (bottoms) at approximately the same price level, suggesting a reversal of the current trend.

B. Continuation Patterns:

A continuation pattern suggests that the current trend will continue after a period of consolidation.

Triangles: Formed by converging trendlines. They can be ascending, descending, or symmetrical and indicate a potential breakout in the direction of the prior trend.

Flags and Pennants: Short-term patterns that show a brief consolidation before the previous trend resumes. Flags are rectangular-shaped, while pennants are small symmetrical triangles.

C. Using Chart Patterns:

Pattern Recognition: Identifying these patterns on price charts can help traders anticipate potential price movements.

Breakout Trading: Traders often enter positions when the price breaks out of the identified pattern, signaling the start of a new trend or the continuation of the existing trend.

COMBINING FUNDAMENTAL AND TECHNICAL ANALYSIS

1. INTEGRATED ANALYSIS

Combining both fundamental and technical analysis provides a more comprehensive view of the oil market. While fundamental analysis helps understand the underlying factors influencing supply and demand, technical analysis offers insights into price movements and market sentiment.

Trade Validation: Fundamental factors, such as geopolitical events, economic data, and supply-demand dynamics, can trigger significant market movements. Technical analysis can help validate these movements by identifying key levels and patterns that confirm the fundamental outlook.

Enhanced Strategies: Traders can develop more robust trading strategies by integrating both analyses. For instance, if a geopolitical event suggests a potential supply disruption (fundamental analysis), traders can look for technical indicators that confirm the expected price movement, such as a breakout above a resistance level.

Example Scenario:

Geopolitical Event: An unexpected conflict in a major oil-producing region leads to concerns about supply disruptions.

Fundamental Analysis: Traders expect oil prices to rise due to potential supply shortages.

Technical Analysis: Traders identify a bullish chart pattern, such as an ascending triangle, and look for a breakout above the resistance level to confirm the anticipated price increase.

Integrated Trade Decision: Combining the fundamental expectation of rising prices with the technical confirmation of a breakout, traders decide to enter a long position.

2. CONFIRMATION SIGNALS

Cross-Verification:

Reducing False Signals: Using technical indicators to confirm fundamental insights can reduce the risk of false signals and improve trade accuracy. For example, if fundamental analysis suggests an increase in oil demand, traders can use moving averages or momentum indicators to confirm the trend before entering a trade.

Timing the Market: Fundamental analysis may indicate a long-term trend, but technical analysis can help pinpoint the best entry and exit points. This allows traders to optimize their trade timing and maximize potential profits.

Contradictory Signals: If technical analysis contradicts fundamental expectations, traders may reconsider or delay their trade. For example, if a bullish fundamental outlook is not supported by technical indicators (e.g., bearish RSI divergence), traders may wait for further confirmation before taking action.

Example Scenario:

Fundamental Insight: Economic reports indicate strong growth in an emerging market, suggesting increased oil demand.

Technical Indicator: The RSI shows that oil prices are currently overbought, signaling a potential short-term correction.

Trade Decision: Traders may wait for the RSI to return to neutral levels before entering a long position, aligning their fundamental expectation with a more favorable technical setup.

Technical analysis provides oil traders with valuable tools and insights to analyze price trends, identify patterns, and make informed trading decisions based on historical price data and market indicators.

By utilizing charts, technical indicators, and patterns, traders can enhance their ability to predict future price movements and execute profitable trades in the dynamic oil market. However, technical analysis should be complemented by fundamental analysis and robust risk management strategies to navigate market uncertainties and achieve long-term trading success.

CHAPTER 12: SENTIMENT ANALYSIS IN OIL TRADING

Sentiment analysis involves assessing the mood, emotions, and opinions of market participants towards an asset or market. In oil trading, sentiment analysis aims to gauge market sentiment and investor psychology to anticipate future price movements and trading opportunities.

SOURCES OF MARKET SENTIMENT

1. NEWS AND MEDIA OUTLETS

Coverage: Monitoring news articles, reports, and commentary from reputable sources covering geopolitical events, economic data releases, and policy developments impacting oil markets.

Sentiment Indicators: Analyzing sentiment indicators derived from media sentiment analysis tools, which quantify positive, negative, or neutral sentiments towards oil-related news.

2. SOCIAL MEDIA AND FORUMS

Real-Time Feedback: Tracking discussions, tweets, and posts on social media platforms and forums (e.g., Twitter, StockTwits, Reddit) to capture retail investor sentiment and market chatter.

Sentiment Analysis Tools: Utilizing sentiment analysis algorithms to aggregate and analyze sentiment scores from social media data, providing insights into public sentiment trends.

3. ANALYST REPORTS AND MARKET COMMENTARIES

Expert Opinions: Reviewing analyst reports, market commentaries, and research publications from financial institutions, investment banks, and industry experts regarding oil price forecasts and market outlooks.

Consensus Estimates: Assessing consensus estimates and recommendations from analysts regarding future oil price trends and market sentiment.

SENTIMENT ANALYSIS TECHNIQUES

1. QUANTITATIVE SENTIMENT INDICATORS

NLP Techniques: Natural Language Processing (NLP) techniques are employed to analyze textual data from various sources such as news articles, social media posts, and financial reports. These techniques classify the text as positive, negative, or neutral.

Score Calculation: Sentiment scores are calculated by assigning numerical values to the classified sentiments. For example, positive sentiments may be given a score of +1, negative sentiments a score of -1, and neutral sentiments a score of 0.

Example Use: If a significant number of news articles report positively on oil market conditions, the aggregated sentiment score would be high, indicating bullish sentiment in the market.

AGGREGATE SENTIMENT INDICES:

Data Aggregation: Sentiment data from various sources is aggregated to form a comprehensive index that reflects the overall market sentiment toward oil prices.

Index Construction: These indices can be constructed by averaging sentiment scores over a specified period and normalizing them to create a consistent and comparable measure.

Market Insight: An aggregate sentiment index helps traders understand the general mood of the market, providing insights into potential market movements driven by collective sentiment.

2. MARKET SENTIMENT CHARTS AND GRAPHS

Sentiment Trends: Sentiment trends are visualized using charts and graphs to track changes in sentiment over time. These visual tools help identify patterns, spikes, or drops in sentiment.

Pattern Analysis: By analyzing sentiment trends, traders can spot periods of increasing or decreasing sentiment, which may correspond to upcoming price movements or market shifts.

Sentiment-Driven Movements: For instance, a sudden increase in positive sentiment might precede a rally in oil prices, while a decline in sentiment could indicate a potential drop in prices.

SENTIMENT ANALYSIS TOOLS AND PLATFORMS

1. SENTIMENT ANALYSIS SOFTWARE

Text Mining Tools: Text mining tools extract relevant textual data from sources like news websites, social media platforms, and financial blogs. These tools use NLP to process and analyze the extracted text.

Sentiment Classification: The software classifies the text into positive, negative, or neutral categories based on predefined algorithms and sentiment dictionaries.

Application: Traders use these tools to stay informed about market sentiment in real-time, helping them make data-driven trading decisions.

SENTIMENT DASHBOARD:

Real-Time Monitoring: Sentiment dashboards provide real-time monitoring of sentiment scores and trends, offering traders a quick overview of market sentiment.

Sentiment Trends and Alerts: These platforms display sentiment trends and can generate alerts based on significant changes in sentiment, helping traders react promptly to market developments.

Comprehensive Analysis: Sentiment dashboards often integrate data from multiple sources, providing a comprehensive view of sentiment across the oil market. This enables traders to corroborate sentiment with other technical and fundamental analysis tools for more informed decision-making

INTEGRATING SENTIMENT ANALYSIS WITH TRADING STRATEGIES

1. SENTIMENT-BASED TRADING SIGNALS

Contrarian Trading: Contrarian traders use sentiment extremes as signals to take positions opposite to the prevailing sentiment. For example, when sentiment becomes excessively bullish (indicating overbuying), contrarians may anticipate a market correction and initiate short positions.

Risk Management: Contrarian trading involves careful risk management due to the potential for sentiment to persist longer than expected. Traders use stop-loss orders and risk-reward ratios to manage trades effectively.

Confirmation Signals: Sentiment analysis is integrated with technical and fundamental analysis to confirm trading signals. For instance, if sentiment data shows strong bullish sentiment and technical indicators like moving averages confirm an uptrend, traders may consider entering a long position.

By corroborating sentiment with other analysis methods, traders increase their confidence in trade decisions, reducing the risk of false signals.

2. EVENT-DRIVEN TRADING STRATEGIES

News Trading: News traders react swiftly to sentiment-driven news events affecting oil markets. Positive or negative news can trigger rapid price movements, offering short-term trading opportunities for traders who can act quickly.

News trading involves employing fast execution strategies and risk management techniques to capitalize on price volatility and avoid slippage. Traders assess the impact of news on sentiment and market sentiment trends, adjusting their positions accordingly.

Sentiment-Based Allocations: Traders adjust portfolio allocations based on prevailing sentiment trends and sentiment-driven market conditions. For example, if sentiment indicates a bullish outlook, traders may increase exposure to oil-related assets.

Adjustments in portfolio allocations consider risk exposures and diversification strategies to manage overall portfolio risk effectively. Sentiment-based allocations can be part of a broader investment strategy aimed at optimizing returns while balancing risk across different market conditions.

Sentiment analysis provides oil traders with valuable insights into market sentiment, investor psychology, and sentiment-driven price dynamics in oil markets. By monitoring news, social media, analyst reports, and sentiment indicators, traders can gauge market sentiment trends, anticipate price movements, and adjust trading strategies accordingly.

However, sentiment analysis should be used in conjunction with technical and fundamental analysis to validate trading signals and mitigate risks effectively.

PART 5: TRADING PLATFORMS AND TOOLS

CHAPTER 13: CHOOSING THE RIGHT TRADING PLATFORM

A trading platform is a software application provided by financial institutions and brokers that allows traders to execute trades, access market data, analyze financial markets, and manage trading accounts.

The choice of a trading platform is crucial for efficient and effective oil trading. It impacts trade execution speed, market access, analysis capabilities, and overall trading experience.

KEY FEATURES OF TRADING PLATFORMS

1. User Interface and Ease of Use

A user-friendly interface with easy navigation, customizable layouts, and efficient order placement features ensures that traders can manage their activities seamlessly. Compatibility with various devices (e.g., desktop, web, mobile) is crucial to facilitate trading from anywhere. This allows traders to monitor markets and execute trades on-the-go, ensuring they never miss an opportunity due to lack of access.

2. Order Execution and Speed

Ensuring trades are executed promptly is particularly important in fast-moving oil markets. Low-latency execution reduces the risk of slippage and ensures that traders can capitalize on market movements as they occur. Availability of various order types, including market orders, limit orders, stop-loss orders, and trailing stops, to implement diverse trading strategies.

3. Charting and Technical Analysis Tools

Comprehensive charting capabilities with multiple timeframes, drawing tools, and customizable indicators. Access to a wide range of technical indicators (e.g., moving averages, RSI, MACD) to support detailed market analysis.

4. Fundamental Analysis Resources

Real-time news feeds and economic calendars to stay updated on market-moving events and data releases. Access to analyst reports, market commentaries, and fundamental data to support informed trading decisions.

5. Risk Management Tools

Tools for setting stop-loss orders, take-profit levels, and position sizing to manage trading risk effectively. Features to monitor portfolio performance, assess risk exposure, and adjust positions as needed.

6. Trading Instruments and Market Access

Availability of various trading instruments, including oil futures, options, CFDs, and ETFs, to diversify trading strategies. Direct market access (DMA) to major exchanges and liquidity providers for optimal trade execution.

7. Customer Support and Education

Reliable customer support with multiple contact channels (e.g., phone, email, chat) to address technical issues and inquiries. Access to educational materials, webinars, and tutorials to enhance trading knowledge and skills.

EVALUATING TRADING PLATFORMS

1. Broker Reputation and Regulation

Choosing platforms offered by brokers regulated by reputable financial authorities (e.g., SEC, FCA, CySEC) to ensure security and transparency. Researching broker reviews, customer feedback, and industry reputation to assess reliability and trustworthiness.

2. Platform Fees and Costs

Understanding commission fees, spreads, and transaction costs associated with the trading platform. Identifying any additional fees, such as withdrawal fees, inactivity fees, and data subscription costs.

3. Platform Stability and Reliability

Evaluating platform uptime, stability, and performance during high volatility periods to ensure seamless trading. Ensuring robust security measures, including encryption, two-factor authentication, and data protection protocols.

4. Demo Accounts and Trial Periods

Utilizing demo accounts or trial periods to test the platform's features, usability, and performance without risking real capital. Practicing trading strategies and familiarizing oneself with platform functionalities using virtual funds.

POPULAR TRADING PLATFORMS FOR OIL TRADING

1. METATRADER 4/5 (MT4/MT5)

Features: Extensive range of charting tools and technical indicators to analyze market trends and price movements. Supports automated trading through Expert Advisors (EAs), allowing traders to develop, test, and apply automated strategies.

MT4 / MT5 Trading Platform: cmcmarkets.com.

Intuitive interface that caters to both novice and experienced traders. Offers the ability to trade a variety of asset classes including oil, forex, stocks, and commodities.

Community: Large and active community of traders sharing strategies, insights, and plugins. Access to a vast library of third-party plugins and custom indicators, enhancing trading capabilities.

2. TRADINGVIEW

Charting Excellence: Comprehensive set of technical analysis tools and indicators to help traders analyze price action and identify trading opportunities.

Pine Script allows traders to create and share custom indicators and strategies. Integrated social network where traders can share ideas, charts, and strategies.

Web-Based: Fully web-based platform, accessible via web browsers on any device, making it convenient for traders who prefer not to download and install software. Extensive coverage of market data across various asset classes, including real-time data and historical price charts.

CHAPTER 13: CHOOSING THE RIGHT TRADING PLATFORM | 77

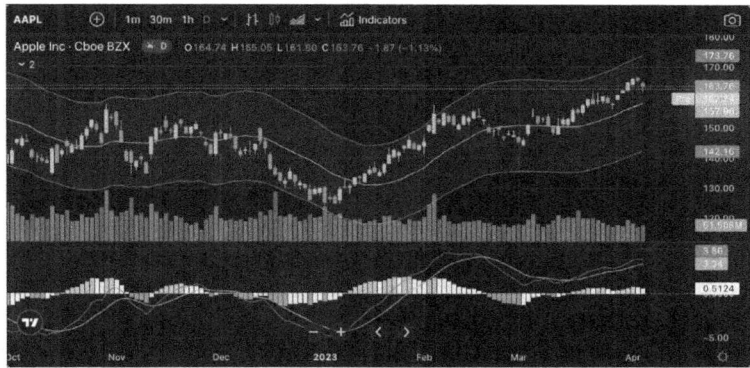

TradingView Desktop Application: tradingview.com

3. THINKORSWIM BY TD AMERITRADE

Comprehensive Tools: High-quality charting capabilities with numerous technical indicators and drawing tools. Tools to manage and analyze risk, including probability analysis and stress testing. Access to in-depth research, market news, and analyst reports to inform trading decisions.

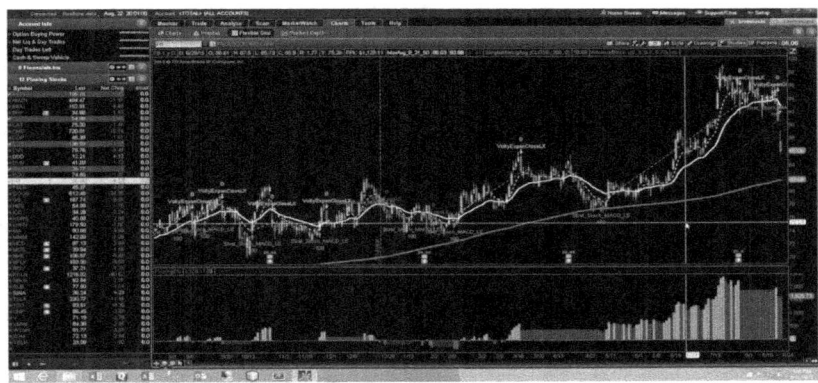

Thinkorswim: hahn-tech.com

Integration: Seamless integration with TD Ameritrade brokerage accounts, allowing for efficient account management and trade execution. Extensive educational content, including webinars, tutorials, and trading guides for continuous learning.

4. INTERACTIVE BROKERS TRADER WORKSTATION (TWS)

Professional Platform: Offers a range of advanced trading tools, including direct market access, sophisticated order types, and algorithmic trading features. Ability to trade a diverse set of instruments including futures, options, stocks, and forex. Comprehensive market data feeds and research tools to support informed trading decisions.

Trader Workstation: interactivebrokers.com

Customization: Highly customizable interface to meet the specific needs of professional and institutional traders. Provides API access for developers to build custom trading applications and integrate with other systems.

These trading platforms are popular among oil traders due to their robust features, advanced analysis tools, and user-friendly interfaces. Each platform caters to different trading styles and preferences, providing essential tools and resources to help traders succeed in the volatile oil markets.

Choosing the right trading platform is a critical decision for oil traders, impacting their trading efficiency, analysis capabilities, and overall trading experience. By evaluating key features such as user interface, order execution, charting tools, fundamental analysis resources, risk management tools, and market access, traders can select a platform that best suits their trading style and objectives.

Additionally, considering factors like broker reputation, regulatory compliance, fees, platform stability, and customer support ensures a secure and reliable trading environment.

CHAPTER 14: ESSENTIAL TOOLS FOR OIL TRADERS

In the dynamic and fast-paced world of oil trading, having the right tools at your disposal is crucial for success. Trading tools encompass a broad range of software applications, resources, and technologies designed to assist traders in analyzing markets, executing trades, managing risk, and enhancing overall trading efficiency. These tools play a vital role in improving decision-making, enabling traders to identify opportunities and manage risks effectively.

In this chapter, we will explore the essential tools every oil trader should consider integrating into their workflow. We will delve into analytical tools, execution and risk management systems, communication and collaboration platforms, and specialized tools tailored for the oil market. Additionally, we will discuss the importance of customizing toolkits to fit individual trading styles and the need for continuous learning and adaptation in the ever-evolving trading landscape.

ANALYTICAL TOOLS

1. TECHNICAL ANALYSIS SOFTWARE

Charting Platforms: Platforms like MetaTrader, TradingView, and Thinkorswim provide advanced charting capabilities, including customizable indicators, drawing tools, and real-time data feeds. These platforms allow traders to perform detailed technical analysis, identify trends, and spot potential trading opportunities.

Backtesting Tools: Software such as MetaTrader's Strategy Tester and TradingView's Pine Script allow traders to test their trading strategies against historical data. This helps evaluate the effectiveness and reliability of strategies before applying them in live trading environments, reducing the risk of unforeseen losses.

2. FUNDAMENTAL ANALYSIS RESOURCES

News Aggregators: Platforms like Bloomberg, Reuters, and Investing.com offer real-time news feeds, economic calendars, and expert market analysis. These resources are essential for staying informed about market-moving events, economic indicators, and geopolitical developments that impact oil prices.

Data Providers: Access to comprehensive data from sources such as the U.S. Energy Information Administration (EIA), the International Energy Agency (IEA), and financial databases is crucial for conducting fundamental analysis. These providers offer detailed reports on oil production, inventory levels, consumption patterns, and other key economic indicators.

3. SENTIMENT ANALYSIS TOOLS

Social Media Monitoring: Tools like Sentimentrader and TradeFeedr analyze sentiment from social media platforms, forums, and news articles to gauge market sentiment and investor psychology. This information can be invaluable for anticipating market movements based on public sentiment.

Sentiment Indicators: Specialized indicators, such as the Bullish/Bearish Sentiment Index, aggregate sentiment data from various sources. These indicators provide insights into the overall market mood, helping traders predict potential price movements and market reversals.

EXECUTION AND RISK MANAGEMENT TOOLS

1. ORDER MANAGEMENT SYSTEMS (OMS)

Order Placement: Order Management Systems (OMS) streamline the process of placing, modifying, and canceling orders across multiple exchanges and trading venues. These systems ensure efficient and accurate order execution, minimizing delays and errors.

Automated Trading: Tools like MetaTrader's Expert Advisors (EAs) and other algorithmic trading software facilitate automated trading. These tools execute trading strategies based on predefined criteria, allowing for high-frequency trading and reducing the emotional aspect of trading decisions.

2. RISK MANAGEMENT SOFTWARE

Position Sizing Calculators: Tools such as Risk Calculator and Myfxbook's Position Size Calculator help traders determine optimal position sizes based on their account size, risk tolerance, and market volatility. This ensures that traders do not over-leverage and can manage risk effectively.

Stop-Loss and Take-Profit Management: Automated tools and scripts can set and adjust stop-loss and take-profit levels. These tools help protect against adverse market movements by locking in profits and limiting potential losses.

3. PORTFOLIO MANAGEMENT TOOLS

Performance Tracking: Software like Myfxbook and TradeStation track the performance of trades, analyzing profitability, drawdowns, and risk-adjusted returns. This helps traders understand their trading performance and make data-driven improvements.

Diversification Analysis: Tools like Portfolio Visualizer and Morningstar's Portfolio X-Ray evaluate portfolio diversification. They help traders spread risk across different assets and markets, ensuring a balanced and risk-mitigated portfolio.

COMMUNICATION AND COLLABORATION TOOLS

1. TRADING COMMUNITIES

Forums and Groups: Online platforms like Reddit's r/wallstreetbets, StockTwits, and specialized trading forums are essential for traders to share insights, strategies, and market updates. These communities provide a space for discussing market trends, technical analysis, and potential trade opportunities.

Professional Networks: Membership in professional networks and associations, such as the Market Technicians Association (MTA) or the CFA Institute, provides access to industry experts, webinars, and educational resources. These networks offer valuable connections and up-to-date information on industry best practices.

2. RESEARCH AND COLLABORATION PLATFORMS

Shared Research Tools: Platforms like Bloomberg Terminal, Refinitiv Eikon, and FactSet allow teams to collaborate on research, share data, and conduct joint analysis. These tools foster a collaborative trading environment, enabling teams to make well-informed decisions.

Cloud-Based Tools: Cloud storage and collaboration tools such as Google Drive, Microsoft OneDrive, and Dropbox are crucial for sharing documents, data, and analysis within a trading team. These tools facilitate real-time collaboration, ensuring that all team members have access to the latest information and can contribute to the trading strategy.

5. EDUCATION AND TRAINING TOOLS

1. ONLINE COURSES AND TUTORIALS

Educational Platforms: Websites like Coursera, Udemy, and Khan Academy offer a wide range of courses covering technical analysis, fundamental analysis, risk management, and trading psychology. These platforms provide structured learning paths and are accessible to traders of all levels.

Webinars and Seminars: Live and recorded webinars hosted by industry experts, brokers, and trading institutions provide valuable insights into market trends, trading strategies, and economic forecasts. Webinars offer interactive learning experiences, allowing traders to ask questions and engage with the presenters.

2. TRADING SIMULATORS

Demo Accounts: Platforms like MetaTrader, TradingView, and Thinkorswim offer demo accounts where traders can practice trading with virtual funds. These accounts allow traders to gain experience, test strategies, and understand market dynamics without risking real capital.

Simulation Software: Advanced trading simulators like NinjaTrader and Wall Street Survivor replicate real market conditions, providing a realistic environment for traders to hone their skills. These simulators help traders build confidence, develop strategies, and improve their decision-making process in a risk-free setting.

SPECIALIZED OIL TRADING TOOLS

1. ENERGY MARKET PLATFORMS

Dedicated Platforms: These are specialized software solutions designed specifically for energy markets, including crude oil, natural gas, and other energy commodities. Examples include ICE (Intercontinental Exchange) and CME Group platforms, which offer robust tools for market analysis, trading, and data management tailored to the energy sector.

Energy Data Providers: Access to detailed and specialized energy data is crucial for making informed trading decisions. Providers like Baker Hughes (for rig counts), EIA (Energy Information Administration), and Platts offer comprehensive data on rig counts, refinery utilization rates, production forecasts, and shipping information. This data helps traders understand supply dynamics, track industry trends, and anticipate market movements.

2. PRICING AND ARBITRAGE TOOLS

Price Comparison Tools: Software that allows traders to compare oil prices across different exchanges and regions. Tools like Thomson Reuters Eikon and Bloomberg Terminal offer price comparison features that highlight arbitrage opportunities, where price discrepancies can be exploited for profit.

Arbitrage Platforms: These tools facilitate the execution of arbitrage strategies by continuously monitoring price discrepancies between markets and automating trades. Platforms such as QuantConnect and 3Commas can be programmed to execute arbitrage strategies efficiently, reducing the time and effort required for manual trading.

INTEGRATING TOOLS INTO A TRADING WORKFLOW

1. CUSTOMIZING TOOLKITS

Personalization: Traders should select and customize their tools based on their specific trading style, preferences, and market focus. This might involve configuring charting software to display preferred technical indicators, setting up automated alerts for specific price movements, or integrating data feeds from preferred news sources.

Integration: Ensuring seamless integration between different tools is essential for an efficient workflow. For instance, integrating charting software with an order management system (OMS) and risk management tools allows for smooth execution of trades, real-time monitoring of positions, and effective management of risk. Tools like APIs (Application Programming Interfaces) and custom software solutions can facilitate this integration.

2. CONTINUOUS LEARNING AND ADAPTATION

Staying Updated: Regularly updating tools and software is crucial to leverage new features, improvements, and bug fixes. Staying current with the latest versions ensures that traders have access to the most advanced functionalities and security features.

Adaptation: The trading environment is constantly evolving, and traders must continuously evaluate and adapt their toolkits to keep up with changing market conditions, trading performance, and evolving strategies. This might involve incorporating new tools, tweaking existing setups, or abandoning outdated methods in favor of more effective solutions.

Integrating these tools into a cohesive trading workflow, while continuously updating and adapting to new developments, ensures traders are well-equipped to navigate the complexities of oil trading and achieve their trading objectives.

CHAPTER 15: USING TRADING SOFTWARE AND APPS

In the modern trading environment, software and mobile applications have become indispensable tools for traders, offering unparalleled convenience, speed, and efficiency. These technologies enable traders to access real-time market data, execute trades swiftly, manage their portfolios, and analyze market trends from anywhere in the world. Whether you are a seasoned professional or a novice trader, leveraging the power of trading software and apps can significantly enhance your trading capabilities.

This chapter will guide you through the various types of trading software and applications available, focusing on their features, functionalities, and benefits. We will explore desktop trading platforms known for their advanced analytical tools and customizability, as well as mobile apps that provide the flexibility to trade on-the-go.

Additionally, we will examine how to choose the right software and apps to suit your trading style and needs, ensuring that you can make the most of these technological advancements.

INTRODUCTION TO TRADING SOFTWARE AND APPS

These are digital platforms and applications designed to facilitate trading activities, provide market analysis tools, and help traders manage their portfolios on various devices including desktops, tablets, and smartphones.

Convenience and Efficiency: Trading software and apps enable traders to access the markets, execute trades, and monitor their portfolios in real-time from anywhere.

Competitive Advantage: Leveraging sophisticated tools and features within trading software and apps can significantly enhance a trader's ability to make informed decisions and act swiftly.

KEY FEATURES OF TRADING SOFTWARE AND APPS

Incorporating these key features into trading software and apps significantly enhances the trader's ability to analyze the market, execute trades efficiently, manage risk effectively, and adapt to the fast-paced dynamics of the oil market.

1. REAL-TIME MARKET DATA AND ANALYSIS

Live Quotes: Access to real-time price quotes and comprehensive market data is essential for making accurate and timely trading decisions. This feature ensures that traders are always updated with the latest market movements and price fluctuations.

Market News and Alerts: Integration with reliable news feeds and customizable alert systems keeps traders informed about significant market events and developments that can impact oil prices. This allows for quick reactions to news that may affect trading strategies.

2. CHARTING AND TECHNICAL ANALYSIS TOOLS

Interactive Charts: Advanced charting capabilities offer traders the ability to view price movements across multiple timeframes with a variety of drawing tools and technical indicators. This enables detailed analysis and helps in identifying trends and potential trade opportunities.

Pattern Recognition: Automated recognition of chart patterns such as head and shoulders, triangles, and double tops/bottoms aids traders in spotting significant patterns that could indicate future price movements, enhancing their ability to capitalize on these opportunities.

3. ORDER EXECUTION AND MANAGEMENT

Order Types: A wide range of order types, including market, limit, stop-loss, and trailing stop orders, provides traders with the flexibility to implement various trading strategies and manage their trades effectively.

One-Click Trading: Features that allow for the quick execution of trades with minimal delay are crucial for capturing fast-moving market opportunities, especially in the highly volatile oil market.

4. RISK MANAGEMENT FEATURES

Risk Controls: Tools that enable traders to set stop-loss and take-profit levels, manage position sizes, and monitor overall risk exposure help in maintaining disciplined trading practices and protecting capital.

Portfolio Analytics: Detailed analytics tools assess portfolio performance, track gains and losses, and evaluate risk-adjusted returns, providing traders with insights into their trading effectiveness and areas for improvement.

5. CUSTOMIZATION AND USER EXPERIENCE

Customizable Interface: The ability to customize layouts, dashboards, and watchlists allows traders to tailor the platform to their individual preferences and workflows, enhancing efficiency and ease of use.

User-Friendly Design: An intuitive design and easy navigation improve the overall user experience, reducing the learning curve and making the software accessible to traders of all experience levels.

6. MOBILE TRADING

Accessibility: Mobile apps that offer full trading functionality on smartphones and tablets provide the flexibility to trade from anywhere, ensuring that traders can monitor and manage their positions on-the-go.

Synchronization: Seamless synchronization between desktop and mobile platforms ensures that all trading activities and data are consistent and up-to-date across all devices, providing a cohesive trading experience.

INTEGRATING TRADING SOFTWARE AND APPS INTO YOUR STRATEGY

1. SETTING UP AND CUSTOMIZING YOUR PLATFORM

Initial Setup:

Download and Installation: Begin by downloading the trading software or app from the official website or app store. Follow the installation prompts to set up the software on your device.

Account Creation: Create an account by providing necessary details such as email, password, and personal information. Complete the verification process, which may include submitting identification documents.

Connecting Your Brokerage Account: Link your trading software to your brokerage account to enable seamless trading. Follow the instructions provided by the platform to authorize the connection.

Customization:

Interface Customization: Personalize the layout of the platform to suit your trading style. Arrange charts, watchlists, and trading tools in a way that enhances your workflow and accessibility.

Setting Up Watchlists: Create and manage watchlists to keep track of your favorite oil assets and other commodities. Organize them based on sectors, trading strategies, or other criteria.

Configuring Alerts: Set up custom alerts to notify you of significant market events, price movements, or technical indicator signals. This ensures you stay informed and can react promptly to market changes.

2. LEVERAGING ANALYTICAL TOOLS

Technical Analysis:

Using Charting Tools: Utilize advanced charting features to analyze price movements. Apply various chart types (e.g., candlestick, bar, line) and customize timeframes to gain different perspectives on market trends.

Applying Technical Indicators: Incorporate indicators such as moving averages, RSI, MACD, and Bollinger Bands to identify trends, overbought/oversold conditions, and potential reversal points.

Drawing Tools: Use drawing tools to mark support and resistance levels, trendlines, and chart patterns. This visual aid helps in recognizing key market structures and planning trades accordingly.

Fundamental Analysis:

Integrated News Feeds: Access real-time news feeds directly within the platform to stay updated on market-moving events and economic developments affecting oil prices.

Economic Calendars: Use economic calendars to track upcoming data releases, such as inventory reports and OPEC meetings, which can influence market sentiment and price movements.

Research Resources: Leverage research tools and reports provided by the platform to gain insights into market conditions, company performance, and industry trends.

3. AUTOMATING YOUR TRADING

Algorithmic Trading:

Creating Automated Strategies: Develop automated trading strategies using expert advisors (EAs) or custom scripts. These algorithms can execute trades based on predefined criteria, reducing the need for manual intervention.

Deploying Strategies: Once created, deploy your automated strategies on the platform. Monitor their performance and make adjustments as necessary to optimize results.

Backtesting:

Historical Data Testing: Use backtesting tools to simulate your trading strategies on historical market data. This helps evaluate the effectiveness and reliability of your strategies under different market conditions.

Performance Analysis: Analyze the results of backtests to understand the strengths and weaknesses of your strategies. Pay attention to key metrics such as profit, drawdown, win rate, and risk-adjusted returns.

Optimization: Refine and optimize your strategies based on backtest results. Adjust parameters and settings to improve performance before applying the strategies in live trading.

By effectively integrating trading software and apps into your trading strategy, you can enhance your ability to analyze markets, execute trades, and manage risks efficiently. Customizing your platform, leveraging analytical tools, and automating your trading processes are essential steps to gaining a competitive edge and improving overall trading performance in the dynamic oil market.

BEST PRACTICES FOR USING TRADING SOFTWARE AND APPS

Regular Updates and Maintenance

Software Updates: Keeping your trading software and apps updated to access the latest features, security patches, and performance improvements.

Data Backup: Regularly backing up your trading data, settings, and customizations to prevent data loss and ensure continuity.

Security Measures

Account Security: Implementing strong passwords, two-factor authentication (2FA), and secure login practices to protect your trading account.

Device Security: Ensuring that your devices (desktop, tablet, smartphone) are protected with antivirus software and secure network connections.

Continuous Learning and Adaptation

Staying Informed: Regularly participating in webinars, tutorials, and online courses to stay updated on new features and best practices.

Adapting to Market Changes: Continuously evaluating and adjusting your trading strategies and tools based on evolving market conditions and trading performance.

Trading software and apps are indispensable tools for modern oil traders, offering a wide range of features and functionalities that enhance market analysis, trade execution, and risk management. By choosing the right platforms, customizing them to suit individual preferences, and leveraging their advanced capabilities, traders can gain a significant edge in the competitive oil markets.

Integrating these tools into a cohesive trading strategy, while adhering to best practices for security and continuous learning, ensures that traders are well-equipped to navigate the complexities of oil trading and achieve their trading objectives.

PART 6: DEVELOPING A TRADING STRATEGY

CHAPTER 16: SETTING TRADING GOALS

Setting trading goals is a crucial step in developing a successful trading strategy. Just as in any endeavor, having clear, well-defined objectives provides direction, motivation, and a framework for evaluating progress. In the fast-paced and often volatile world of oil trading, establishing realistic and achievable goals helps traders maintain focus, discipline, and emotional control.

This chapter explores the importance of setting trading goals, the types of goals traders should consider, and practical strategies for setting and achieving these goals. Whether you're aiming for consistent profitability, risk management, or personal development, understanding how to set and pursue your trading goals can significantly enhance your trading performance and overall success in the markets.

INTRODUCTION TO TRADING GOALS

Setting clear and achievable trading goals is fundamental to success in the dynamic world of oil trading. These goals not only provide direction and purpose but also serve as benchmarks for evaluating progress and improving performance over time. Whether you're aiming to maximize profits, manage risks effectively, or enhance your trading skills, having well-defined goals can significantly enhance your trading journey.

Trading Goals are Specific, measurable, achievable, relevant, and time-bound (SMART) objectives that traders set to guide their trading activities, manage risk, and achieve long-term success.

Direction and Focus: Trading goals act as a compass, guiding traders through the complexities of the market. They help maintain focus on strategic objectives, preventing distractions and emotional decision-making that can lead to costly mistakes.

Performance Measurement: Goals serve as measurable targets against which traders can assess their performance. By setting benchmarks for profitability, risk management, and other key metrics, traders can objectively evaluate their success and identify areas for improvement.

TYPES OF TRADING GOALS

1. FINANCIAL GOALS

Profit Targets: Establishing specific financial goals, such as achieving a target percentage return on investment (ROI) or a set dollar amount within a defined timeframe. This provides clarity on what constitutes a successful trade or investment period.

Income Generation: Setting goals for generating consistent income from trading activities. This could involve monthly or quarterly income targets, aligning trading strategies with financial needs and objectives.

2. RISK MANAGEMENT GOALS

Loss Limits: Defining maximum acceptable losses per trade, day, week, or month to safeguard capital and mitigate the impact of market volatility. Clear loss limits help maintain financial stability and discipline during adverse market conditions.

Risk-Reward Ratios: Setting goals to maintain favorable risk-reward ratios for trades. This ensures that potential profits justify the risks taken, guiding decision-making towards prudent risk management practices.

3. LEARNING AND DEVELOPMENT GOALS

Skill Improvement: Goals focused on enhancing specific trading skills, such as technical analysis, fundamental analysis, or the use of trading tools and platforms. Continuous skill development empowers traders to adapt to market changes and seize opportunities effectively.

Education and Training: Setting objectives for acquiring knowledge through courses, books, seminars, or workshops. Ongoing education strengthens market understanding and cultivates expertise, enhancing confidence in trading decisions.

4. BEHAVIORAL GOALS

Discipline and Patience: Establishing goals to cultivate disciplined trading habits and patience in executing trading strategies. This includes adhering to trading plans, maintaining consistency in decision-making, and avoiding impulsive actions driven by emotions.

Emotional Control: Setting goals to manage emotional responses such as fear, greed, and frustration, which can influence trading outcomes. Developing emotional resilience fosters a calm and rational approach to trading, improving overall performance and decision-making.

SETTING SMART TRADING GOALS

1. Specific

Clarity: Ensure that trading goals are clear and specific, detailing exactly what is to be achieved and the steps to get there.

Example: Instead of "make more money," a specific goal would be "achieve a 10% return on investment within six months."

2. Measurable

Quantifiable Metrics: Define measurable criteria to track progress and determine when a goal has been achieved.

Example: Set a goal to "limit daily trading losses to 2% of total account equity."

3. Achievable

Realistic Objectives: Set goals that are challenging yet attainable, considering current skills, experience, and resources.

Example: A novice trader might set a goal to "increase trading knowledge by completing two online courses in the next three months."

4. Relevant

Alignment with Trading Strategy: Ensure that goals align with overall trading strategy, risk tolerance, and long-term objectives.

Example: If focusing on swing trading, a relevant goal could be "identify and execute five high-probability swing trades per month."

5. Time-Bound

Deadline: Set a clear timeframe for achieving each goal to create a sense of urgency and facilitate planning.

Example: Establish a goal to "reduce average trade duration to less than one week within the next quarter."

DEVELOPING A TRADING PLAN

Developing a structured trading plan, tracking performance metrics, and maintaining a detailed trading journal, helps you to systematically work towards achieving your trading goals in the competitive oil markets.

1. COMPREHENSIVE TRADING PLAN

A robust trading plan is the foundation of successful trading. It should encompass:

Components: Include detailed strategies for entry and exit points based on technical or fundamental analysis. Define clear risk management rules, such as stop-loss and take-profit levels, to protect capital and optimize trade outcomes. Additionally, outline criteria for evaluating trade performance and adjusting strategies as needed.

Documentation: Documenting your trading plan is crucial. It serves as a reference point to maintain discipline and consistency in trading decisions. Specify your trading goals within the plan, aligning them with your overall financial objectives and risk tolerance.

2. REGULAR REVIEW AND ADJUSTMENT

Ongoing Evaluation: Regularly review your trading plan to assess its effectiveness in achieving your goals. Evaluate market conditions, performance metrics, and adherence to trading rules. Adjust your plan as necessary to adapt to changing market dynamics or refine trading strategies.

Flexibility: Markets evolve, and so should your trading plan. Remain flexible in modifying your goals and strategies based on new insights, emerging trends, or personal circumstances. This adaptability enhances your ability to capitalize on opportunities and mitigate risks effectively.

TRACKING AND EVALUATING PROGRESS

1. PERFORMANCE METRICS

Tracking essential performance metrics is crucial for assessing your trading effectiveness and progress. These metrics include:

Win-Loss Ratio: This metric measures the proportion of winning trades relative to losing trades over a specific period. A higher win-loss ratio indicates a higher percentage of successful trades, reflecting effective trading strategies and decision-making.

Average Profit/Loss per Trade: Evaluating the average financial outcome of your trades helps in understanding the profitability of your trading strategy. It provides insights into how well your trades perform on average, considering both gains and losses.

Drawdown: Assessing drawdown involves measuring the peak-to-trough decline in your trading account's equity during a specified time frame. Monitoring drawdown helps you gauge risk exposure and ensure that losses remain within acceptable limits relative to your trading capital.

Return on Investment (ROI): Calculating ROI allows you to determine the profitability of your trades relative to the capital invested. It quantifies the efficiency of your trading strategy in generating returns and helps in comparing performance across different investment opportunities.

Utilize these metrics to monitor progress towards your trading goals. Analyze trends in performance metrics to identify strengths and weaknesses in your trading approach. By focusing on data-driven insights, you can adjust your strategies to enhance overall performance and achieve your objectives more effectively.

2. JOURNALING AND RECORD-KEEPING

Trading Journal:

Maintaining a detailed trading journal is essential for comprehensive record-keeping and analysis. In your journal, document:

Trade Entries and Exits: Record the specifics of each trade, including entry and exit points, trade size, and type of order placed (e.g., market, limit).

Rationale Behind Each Trade: Describe the reasons and analysis that led to each trade decision. Include factors such as technical indicators, fundamental analysis, and market sentiment.

Market Conditions: Note the prevailing market conditions at the time of trade execution, including volatility, trends, and any significant news events influencing price movements.

Emotional Factors: Reflect on your emotional state during each trade. Document feelings such as fear, greed, or confidence, as emotions can impact decision-making and trade outcomes.

Analysis:

Regularly review entries in your trading journal to gain insights into your trading behavior and outcomes. Analyze:

Decision-Making Process: Evaluate the effectiveness of your decision-making strategies based on the outcomes of your trades. Identify patterns in your approach to refine and improve your trading strategies.

Emotional Responses: Assess how emotions influenced your trading decisions and outcomes. Recognize patterns of emotional bias and develop strategies to manage emotions effectively.

Adherence to Trading Plan: Measure your adherence to your trading plan and rules. Identify instances where deviations occurred and analyze their impact on performance.

Use this analysis to refine your strategies, enhance discipline, and mitigate recurring mistakes.

PSYCHOLOGICAL ASPECTS OF GOAL SETTING

1. MOTIVATION AND COMMITMENT

Inspiration: Setting meaningful trading goals can serve as a source of inspiration and motivation throughout your trading journey. Clear goals provide a sense of purpose and direction, encouraging perseverance during challenging market conditions.

Accountability: Sharing your goals with a mentor, trading coach, or within a trading community fosters accountability. Accountability partners can provide support, guidance, and constructive feedback to help you stay focused and committed to achieving your objectives.

2. MANAGING EXPECTATIONS

Realistic Expectations: Setting realistic trading goals is essential to maintain psychological well-being and avoid undue stress. Realistic goals consider your experience level, market conditions, and risk tolerance, aligning expectations with achievable outcomes.

Gradual Progress: Acknowledge that trading success often involves gradual progress and continuous learning. Embrace mistakes as opportunities for growth and refinement of your trading skills. By adopting a mindset of gradual improvement, you can navigate setbacks with resilience and persistence.

Setting trading goals is a fundamental aspect of successful oil trading, providing direction, focus, and a framework for measuring progress. By establishing SMART goals, developing a comprehensive trading plan, and regularly tracking performance, traders can enhance their decision-making, manage risks effectively, and achieve their long-term objectives.

Embracing the psychological aspects of goal setting, such as motivation, commitment, and managing expectations, further supports a disciplined and resilient trading mindset.

CHAPTER 17: RISK MANAGEMENT AND POSITION SIZING

Effective risk management and position sizing are fundamental to successful trading in the volatile oil markets. This chapter delves into essential strategies and principles that traders can employ to mitigate risks and optimize their trading positions. By understanding and implementing robust risk management techniques, traders can safeguard their capital, maintain consistency in performance, and enhance long-term profitability.

INTRODUCTION TO RISK MANAGEMENT

Risk management refers to the systematic process of identifying, assessing, and controlling potential losses. It involves implementing strategies and techniques to protect capital from adverse market movements and uncertainties, thereby ensuring sustainable trading performance. Effective risk management is crucial for several reasons:

Capital Preservation: By implementing risk management strategies, traders can safeguard their trading capital. This preservation allows them to remain active in the market and capitalize on future trading opportunities without depleting their resources through significant losses.

Emotional Stability: Managing risk helps traders maintain emotional stability during trading activities. Emotional reactions such as fear and greed can lead to impulsive decisions and erratic trading behavior. With structured risk management in place, traders can reduce stress, maintain discipline, and make rational decisions based on predefined strategies.

KEY CONCEPTS IN RISK MANAGEMENT

Risk-Reward Ratio: This ratio quantifies the potential profit against the potential loss in a trade. A favorable risk-reward ratio ensures that the potential reward justifies the risk undertaken in a trade. For instance, a risk-reward ratio of 1:3 indicates that for every dollar at risk, the trader anticipates making three dollars in potential profit.

Example: Suppose a trader places a trade with a risk of $100. With a risk-reward ratio of 1:3, the expected profit target would be $300, aligning with the risk undertaken.

Maximum Drawdown: This metric measures the largest peak-to-trough decline in the value of a trading account over a specific period. It provides insights into the potential loss a trader could experience from their account's highest point to its lowest, highlighting the risk associated with their trading strategy.

Monitoring maximum drawdown is essential as it helps traders assess the potential downside risk of their trading approach. By understanding and managing drawdown levels, traders can adjust their strategies to minimize losses and protect their capital during adverse market conditions.

Stop-Loss Orders: A stop-loss order is a risk management tool used to limit potential losses on a trade. It instructs a broker to sell a security when it reaches a specified price level, thereby preventing further losses beyond a predetermined threshold.

Implementing stop-loss orders is critical in risk management as it provides traders with a disciplined approach to exiting losing positions. By setting stop-loss levels based on technical or fundamental analysis, traders can protect their capital from unexpected market fluctuations and adverse price movements.

POSITION SIZING

Position sizing is a critical aspect of risk management in trading. It involves determining the appropriate amount of capital to allocate to each trade based on factors such as account size, risk tolerance, and market conditions. This chapter explores various methods of position sizing to help traders effectively manage risk and optimize trading performance.

Position sizing refers to the process of determining the number of units or contracts to trade in each position. It is essential for balancing risk and reward, ensuring that no single trade significantly impacts the overall portfolio. Proper position sizing plays a crucial role in risk management by:

Risk Control: Limiting the amount of capital at risk on any single trade, thereby protecting the trading account from substantial losses.

Portfolio Management: Allowing traders to diversify their portfolio effectively and manage exposure across different assets or markets.

Consistency: Promoting consistency in trading practices, ensuring that traders adhere to predefined risk parameters and trading strategies.

1. Fixed Fractional Position Sizing

Method: Fixed fractional position sizing allocates a fixed percentage of the trading account to each trade. For example, traders commonly risk 1-2% of their account capital per trade.

Example: Suppose a trader has a $10,000 trading account and decides to risk 1% per trade. The maximum amount they would risk on any single trade is $100 ($10,000 * 0.01).

2. Volatility-Based Position Sizing

Method: Volatility-based position sizing adjusts the position size according to market volatility. In more volatile markets, smaller position sizes are used to manage risk effectively, while in less volatile markets, larger positions may be considered.

Calculation: Traders often use indicators like the Average True Range (ATR) to measure market volatility. The ATR helps in determining the appropriate size of positions relative to the current market conditions and volatility levels.

3. Kelly Criterion

The Kelly Criterion is a mathematical formula used to determine the optimal size of a series of bets or trades to maximize the long-term growth of capital.

Calculation: The Kelly percentage is calculated using the formula:

Kelly percentage = $W - [(1 - W) / R]$,

Where W is the win probability and R is the win/loss ratio. This formula helps traders allocate capital proportionally based on the expected return and probability of success for each trade.

Consideration: While the Kelly Criterion can maximize growth over the long term, it also involves higher risk. Therefore, many traders use a fraction of the Kelly percentage to balance risk and reward according to their risk tolerance and trading objectives.

RISK MANAGEMENT TECHNIQUES

1. Diversification

Diversification involves spreading investments across a range of assets or markets to mitigate risk exposure. By not concentrating all investments in a single asset or market, traders can reduce the impact of adverse movements in any one area.

Application: In oil trading, diversification can mean engaging in trades involving various types of oil (such as Brent crude, WTI crude), related commodities (like natural gas or heating oil), or even other asset classes (such as equities or currencies). This approach helps to balance risk and potentially smooth returns.

2. Hedging

Hedging uses financial instruments like options or futures to protect against potential losses in a primary investment. It's akin to taking out insurance on a trade.

Example: An oil trader who is long on crude oil futures might purchase put options as a hedge. If the price of oil declines, the gains from the put options can offset the losses in the futures position, thereby reducing overall risk.

3. Scaling In and Out

Scaling involves gradually entering or exiting trading positions in smaller increments rather than committing to a full position all at once. This method can manage risk by averaging entry and exit prices.

Implementation: Instead of investing in a full position immediately, a trader might start with a partial position and add to it as the market moves favorably. Similarly, a trader may exit positions in stages to lock in profits incrementally and reduce exposure as the market progresses.

4. Regular Risk Assessment

Continuous Evaluation: Effective risk management requires ongoing assessment and adjustment of strategies based on trading performance and evolving market conditions.

Adaptation: Traders should be flexible and willing to modify their risk management techniques as needed, reflecting changes in the market environment, their trading performance, and personal risk tolerance.

PSYCHOLOGICAL ASPECTS OF RISK MANAGEMENT

1. Emotional Discipline

Managing emotions such as fear and greed is crucial to adhering to risk management rules. Emotional discipline helps traders maintain consistent behavior and avoid impulsive decisions.

Techniques: Strategies to cultivate emotional discipline include mindfulness practices, journaling trading activities and emotions, and mentally rehearsing responses to various market scenarios.

2. Avoiding Overtrading

Overtrading happens when traders take too many positions, often driven by impatience or the desire to quickly recover losses. This behavior can lead to increased transaction costs and higher risk exposure.

Prevention: Traders can set strict trading rules, such as limiting the number of trades per day or week. Taking regular breaks and stepping away from the trading screen can also help prevent impulsive trading decisions.

3. Acceptance of Losses

Accepting that losses are an unavoidable part of trading is essential for maintaining a positive and resilient mindset. Understanding that not every trade will be a winner helps traders focus on the long-term success of their strategies.

Perspective: Traders should view losses as valuable learning opportunities. Analyzing losing trades can provide insights into market behavior and highlight areas for improvement in trading strategies and risk management practices.

PRACTICAL STEPS TO IMPLEMENT RISK MANAGEMENT

1. DEVELOP A RISK MANAGEMENT PLAN

Creating a comprehensive risk management plan is crucial for maintaining discipline and consistency in trading. Key components of a solid plan include:

Risk Tolerance Levels: Define how much risk you are willing to take on each trade and overall portfolio risk. This involves setting maximum acceptable loss limits for individual trades and for your total account.

Position Sizing Rules: Establish guidelines for how much capital to allocate to each trade based on your risk tolerance and the trade's risk-reward ratio. Position sizing can be determined using methods like the fixed fractional model, which allocates a fixed percentage of your account to each trade.

Stop-Loss and Take-Profit Strategies: Pre-determine stop-loss orders to automatically sell a position if it reaches a certain loss level, limiting potential losses. Similarly, set take-profit orders to lock in profits when a trade reaches a predetermined profit level.

Contingency Plans: Develop plans for unforeseen events, such as market crashes or technical failures. This might include having backup trading systems or knowing how to reach your broker quickly to close positions.

Documentation: Write down your risk management plan and keep it easily accessible. Regularly review and update the plan to reflect changes in your trading style, market conditions, and risk tolerance. Documenting the plan helps ensure adherence and provides a reference to stay on track.

2. USE TECHNOLOGY AND TOOLS

Software: Leverage advanced trading platforms and risk management software to enhance your risk management efforts. These tools can:

Set Alerts: Configure alerts for price movements, news events, or other triggers that could impact your trades, allowing you to react quickly.

Automate Stop-Loss Orders: Automatically execute stop-loss orders to limit losses without requiring constant monitoring.

Monitor Risk Metrics: Use software to track key risk metrics such as maximum drawdown, value at risk (VaR), and Sharpe ratio, helping you assess the risk profile of your portfolio.

Apps: Utilize mobile apps to stay connected to the markets and manage your trades on the go. Mobile trading apps can:

Provide Real-Time Updates: Receive real-time notifications of market changes, order executions, and risk alerts, enabling you to make informed decisions quickly.

Facilitate Quick Adjustments: Easily adjust trades and risk parameters from anywhere, ensuring you can respond promptly to market movements.

3. CONTINUOUS EDUCATION

Learning: Continuous education is vital for staying ahead in the dynamic world of trading. To keep your risk management skills sharp:

Stay Updated on Best Practices: Regularly engage in courses, webinars, and reading materials that cover risk management techniques, trading strategies, and market analysis.

Explore New Tools: Stay informed about the latest trading tools and technologies that can enhance your risk management capabilities.

Adapt to Evolving Market Conditions: Understand how changing market conditions, such as economic shifts or geopolitical events, can impact your trading and adjust your risk management strategies accordingly.

Networking: Engaging with trading communities and professionals can provide valuable insights and support:

Exchange Ideas: Participate in forums, attend conferences, and join trading groups to discuss strategies, share experiences, and learn from others.

Gain Insights: Networking with experienced traders and industry experts can help you discover effective risk management techniques and stay informed about market trends.

By developing a robust risk management plan, leveraging technology and tools, and committing to continuous education, you can effectively manage risk and enhance your trading success.

Effective risk management and position sizing are essential components of successful oil trading. By understanding key risk management concepts, employing appropriate position sizing methods, and implementing practical risk management techniques, traders can protect their capital, manage emotional challenges, and achieve sustainable trading success.

CHAPTER 18: CREATING A TRADING PLAN

Having a well-structured trading plan is essential for achieving long-term success. A trading plan serves as a comprehensive roadmap, outlining your trading goals, strategies, risk management rules, and performance evaluation criteria. It helps you stay disciplined, make informed decisions, and avoid emotional trading, which can lead to significant losses.

Creating a robust trading plan involves meticulous preparation and a deep understanding of both the markets and your own trading style. By clearly defining your objectives and establishing concrete guidelines, you can navigate the complexities of oil trading with confidence and precision. This chapter will guide you through the process of developing an effective trading plan, covering key components such as goal setting, strategy formulation, risk management, and performance tracking.

INTRODUCTION TO A TRADING PLAN

A Trading Plan is a structured document that outlines a trader's strategy, rules, and guidelines for entering and exiting trades, managing risk, and achieving trading goals.

Discipline and Consistency: A trading plan helps traders stay disciplined and consistent, reducing emotional decision-making and impulsive trading.

Performance Evaluation: Provides a framework for evaluating trading performance, identifying strengths and weaknesses, and making necessary adjustments.

KEY COMPONENTS OF A TRADING PLAN

1. TRADING GOALS

Short-Term Goals

Daily Targets: Define specific profit and loss targets for each trading day. For instance, you might aim to achieve a certain dollar amount or percentage return per day.

Weekly Goals: Set weekly objectives that align with your daily targets, such as a cumulative profit target or limiting weekly losses to a predetermined amount.

Monthly Metrics: Establish monthly goals to track overall performance, including total profits, number of successful trades, and adherence to the trading plan.

Long-Term Goals

Annual Targets: Outline yearly objectives, including total profit goals, growth in account size, and improvement in trading skills.

Career Milestones: Identify significant milestones in your trading career, such as achieving a specific level of expertise, obtaining professional certifications, or reaching a substantial account size.

Overall Objectives: Define broader goals, such as financial independence, consistent profitability, or becoming a full-time trader.

2. MARKET ANALYSIS

Fundamental Analysis

Economic Indicators: Monitor key economic indicators like GDP growth, inflation rates, employment data, and central bank policies that impact oil prices.

Geopolitical Events: Stay informed about geopolitical developments, such as conflicts in oil-producing regions, OPEC decisions, and international trade agreements.

Supply-Demand Factors: Analyze factors affecting supply and demand, including production levels, inventory data, technological advancements, and changes in consumer behavior.

Technical Analysis

Charts and Patterns: Utilize various chart types (e.g., candlestick, bar, line) to identify price trends and patterns like head and shoulders, double tops, and triangles.

Indicators: Apply technical indicators such as moving averages, RSI, MACD, and Bollinger Bands to predict future price movements and confirm trading signals.

Support and Resistance: Identify key support and resistance levels to plan entry and exit points effectively.

Sentiment Analysis

News Analysis: Assess market sentiment by analyzing news reports, expert opinions, and financial commentaries related to oil markets.

Social Media: Track sentiment on social media platforms and trading forums to gauge market mood and investor psychology.

Trader Behavior: Observe behavior patterns of other traders, including trading volume, open interest, and positioning data.

3. TRADING STRATEGY

Entry and Exit Rules: Establish specific criteria for entering and exiting trades based on your analysis. For example, you might enter a trade when a certain technical indicator crosses a threshold or exit when a fundamental factor changes.

Define preferred trade setups, such as buying on pullbacks during an uptrend or shorting on rallies in a downtrend. Set precise triggers for trade execution, ensuring that they are objective and measurable.

Trade Setup: Develop strategies that capitalize on ongoing market trends by buying in uptrends and selling in downtrends. Create strategies that exploit price reversals to the mean after significant deviations. Identify breakout points from established price ranges to capitalize on significant price movements.

Timeframes

Intraday Trading: Focus on short-term trades within a single trading day, capitalizing on small price movements.

Swing Trading: Plan trades that span several days or weeks, aiming to profit from medium-term price trends.

Long-Term Trading: Develop strategies for long-term investments, holding positions for months or years to benefit from major price trends.

4. RISK MANAGEMENT

Define the maximum amount of capital you are willing to risk on a single trade, typically expressed as a percentage of your total account size.

Position Size Calculations: Use position sizing formulas to determine the appropriate size of each trade based on your risk tolerance and the distance to your stop-loss level.

Stop-Loss Orders: Set stop-loss orders at specific price levels to limit potential losses on each trade. Adjust stop-loss levels as the trade progresses to lock in profits and minimize risk.

Risk-Reward Ratio: Establish a minimum risk-reward ratio for your trades, ensuring that the potential reward justifies the risk taken. A common target is a 2:1 or 3:1 ratio. Regularly evaluate the risk-reward ratio of potential trades before execution.

5. PERFORMANCE EVALUATION

Metrics

Win-Loss Ratio: Track the number of winning trades versus losing trades to assess overall trading success.

Average Profit/Loss per Trade: Calculate the average profit and loss per trade to determine the effectiveness of your trading strategy.

Drawdown: Measure the peak-to-trough decline in your account balance to understand the risk of your trading strategy.

Return on Investment (ROI): Calculate the overall return on investment to gauge the profitability of your trading activities.

Review Process

Schedule regular reviews (e.g., weekly, monthly) to evaluate your trading performance and adherence to the trading plan. Analyze trade outcomes, identifying patterns, strengths, and areas for improvement. Make necessary adjustments to your trading plan based on performance review findings.

6. RECORD-KEEPING

Trading Journal: Keep a detailed trading journal where you record every trade meticulously, noting down entry and exit points, your reasoning behind each trade, the outcomes, and the emotions you experienced during the trade. This journal serves as a valuable tool to gain deep insights into your trading behavior, helping you pinpoint strengths and weaknesses. By regularly reviewing your journal, you can identify areas for improvement and refine your trading approach over time.

Documentation: Maintain thorough documentation of your trading activities, including updates and revisions to your trading plan for future reference. Keep historical records of all trades and performance metrics to monitor your progress and evolution as a trader. These records serve as valuable references for analyzing past decisions and improving future strategies.

DEVELOPING A TRADING PLAN

1. Setting Realistic Goals

Specific: Setting Realistic Goals involves creating a structured framework to guide trading activities and ensure progress. Goals should be specific, clear, and well-defined, such as aiming for a 10% return on investment within six months.

Measurable: They must be measurable, providing quantifiable targets to track progress, like limiting daily losses to 2% of total account equity.

Achievable: Goals need to be achievable, taking into account the trader's current skills, experience, and prevailing market conditions.

Relevant: Goals should be time-bound, with set deadlines to create a sense of urgency and facilitate effective planning.

Time-Bound: Deadlines to create a sense of urgency and facilitate planning.

2. Choosing a Trading Strategy

Select a strategy that aligns with trading goals and personal preferences. Test the strategy on historical data to evaluate its effectiveness and make necessary adjustments. Be willing to refine or change the strategy based on performance and market conditions.

3. Defining Risk Management Rules

Determine how much capital you are willing to risk on each trade and overall. Set stop-loss orders at levels that limit losses while allowing room for market fluctuations. Spread investments across different assets or markets to reduce risk exposure.

4. Creating a Routine

Establish a consistent routine for analyzing markets, executing trades, and reviewing performance. Conduct pre-market research and analysis to identify potential trading opportunities. Review and analyze trades, outcomes, and adherence to the trading plan.

IMPLEMENTING AND ADHERING TO THE TRADING PLAN

Execution: Discipline is crucial in trading; it involves adhering strictly to the trading plan and resisting impulsive decisions driven by emotions or market noise. Consistency is equally important; by following the plan consistently, regardless of short-term outcomes, traders can achieve long-term success.

Monitoring and Adjusting: Monitoring and adjusting the trading plan involves regularly reviewing the plan, performance, and market conditions to identify areas for improvement. It also requires being open to making adjustments based on performance data and evolving market conditions.

Psychological Aspects: Managing the psychological aspects of trading is crucial. Traders must control emotions such as fear, greed, and frustration to maintain discipline and consistency. Patience is also essential, allowing the trading plan to work over time and resisting the temptation to make frequent changes.

PRACTICAL EXAMPLE OF A TRADING PLAN

1. Trading Goals

Short-Term Goal: Achieve a 5% return on investment in three months.

Long-Term Goal: Achieve a 20% return on investment in one year.

2. Market Analysis

Fundamental Analysis: Monitor key economic indicators, geopolitical events, and oil inventory reports.

Technical Analysis: Use moving averages, RSI, and MACD for entry and exit signals.

Sentiment Analysis: Track market sentiment through news and social media.

3. Trading Strategy

Entry Rules: Enter trades when the price crosses above the 50-day moving average and RSI is below 70.

Exit Rules: Exit trades when the price crosses below the 50-day moving average or RSI is above 70.

Timeframes: Focus on swing trading with a holding period of several days to weeks.

4. Risk Management

Position Sizing: Risk 1% of total account equity per trade.

Stop-Loss Orders: Set stop-loss orders at 2% below the entry price.

Risk-Reward Ratio: Aim for a minimum risk-reward ratio of 1:3.

5. Performance Evaluation

Evaluate your performance by tracking metrics such as win-loss ratio, average profit/loss per trade, and overall return on investment. Implement a regular review process, ideally on a weekly basis, to assess trades and make necessary adjustments to your trading plan.

6. Record-Keeping

Keep a trading journal to meticulously record all trades, noting entry and exit points, rationale, outcomes, and emotional responses. Additionally, maintain comprehensive documentation that includes your trading plan along with any updates and revisions made over time.

Creating a comprehensive trading plan is crucial for success in oil trading. A well-structured plan helps traders stay disciplined, manage risk, and achieve their trading goals. By setting realistic goals, choosing a suitable trading strategy, defining risk management rules, and adhering to a consistent routine, traders can navigate the complexities of the oil market with confidence and achieve sustainable profitability. Continuous evaluation, adjustment, and psychological discipline further support long-term success in trading.

PART 7: EXECUTING TRADES

CHAPTER 19: PLACING ORDERS

MARKET, LIMIT, STOP-LOSS

Understanding how to effectively place orders is fundamental to navigating the complexities of trading markets. Whether executing trades in fast-moving environments or strategically entering positions, mastering order types such as market orders, limit orders, and stop-loss orders is crucial.

This chapter delves into the nuances of each order type, exploring their functionalities, advantages, and strategic applications. By comprehensively understanding these tools, traders can enhance their precision, manage risk more effectively, and optimize their trading strategies in diverse market conditions.

INTRODUCTION TO ORDER TYPES

Order types are fundamental instructions provided to brokers to facilitate the buying or selling of assets under specified conditions. Mastery of these order types is essential for executing trades with precision and managing associated risks effectively.

Execution Control: Each order type offers distinct advantages in controlling execution parameters. For instance, market orders ensure immediate execution but at potentially fluctuating prices, while limit orders enable precise control over execution prices.

Risk Management: Proper use of order types plays a crucial role in managing risk exposure. Stop-loss orders, for example, are pivotal in limiting potential losses by automatically triggering trades at predetermined price levels, thus protecting trading capital in volatile markets.

1. MARKET ORDERS

A market order is a fundamental type of order in trading that instructs brokers to buy or sell an asset immediately at the prevailing market price. Unlike limit orders, which specify a particular price point for execution, market orders prioritize speed of execution over price certainty. Market orders possess distinct characteristics that cater to traders looking for rapid execution:

Characteristics: Market orders are executed promptly at the best available price in the market at the time the order reaches the trading venue. This ensures swift entry or exit from a position without delay.

One critical consideration with market orders is the potential for price slippage. This occurs when the actual execution price differs from the expected price due to rapid movements in market prices between the time the order is placed and when it is executed. During periods of high volatility or in thinly traded markets, price slippage can be more pronounced.

Usage of Market Orders

Market orders are strategically employed in trading scenarios where swift execution takes precedence over precise pricing considerations. Here's a deeper look into their usage:

Market orders are ideal in situations where immediate execution is paramount, regardless of obtaining the exact market price. Traders often opt for market orders during periods of heightened market volatility or when there is a need to enter or exit positions swiftly to capitalize on emerging opportunities or mitigate risks promptly.

Advantages: The primary advantage of market orders lies in their ability to execute trades swiftly. They are straightforward and ensure that the trade is executed promptly at the prevailing market price without delays. This simplicity makes them suitable for traders seeking quick action without the complexities associated with limit or stop orders.

Disadvantages: Despite their speed and simplicity, market orders carry inherent risks, particularly the potential for price slippage. Price slippage occurs when the actual execution price differs from the expected price due to rapid fluctuations in market prices. This risk is more pronounced during periods of high volatility or in thinly traded markets where liquidity may be limited.

2. LIMIT ORDERS

A limit order is a specific instruction given to a broker to buy or sell an asset at a predetermined price or better.

Characteristics: Limit orders offer traders precise control over the execution price. They ensure that trades are executed only at the specified price or a better price, providing a level of certainty regarding the transaction's cost.

Execution Uncertainty: However, there is no guarantee that a limit order will be filled if the market does not reach the specified price. This uncertainty arises because limit orders are conditional on the market trading at or better than the specified price.

Usage of Limit Orders: Traders employ limit orders when the exact execution price is more critical than immediate trade execution. This approach is advantageous when entering or exiting positions at specific price levels deemed favorable by the trader.

Advantages: The primary advantage of limit orders lies in their ability to control the execution price. By specifying the desired price level, traders can potentially achieve better pricing than the current market price. Moreover, limit orders mitigate the risk of price slippage, which is common with market orders in volatile markets.

Disadvantages: Despite their advantages, limit orders carry the risk of missed trading opportunities. If the market fails to reach the specified price, the order may not be executed, potentially causing traders to miss out on favorable market movements. This risk is particularly relevant in fast-moving markets or during periods of low liquidity.

3. STOP-LOSS ORDERS

A stop-loss order is an instruction given to a broker to buy or sell an asset once its price reaches a specified level, known as the stop price. The primary purpose of a stop-loss order is to limit potential losses on a position.

Characteristics: Stop-loss orders play a crucial role in risk management by helping traders protect their trading capital. By setting a stop price, traders define the maximum amount they are willing to lose on a trade.

Trigger Price: When the market price reaches or falls below the stop price, the stop-loss order is triggered. It then becomes a market order, executed at the best available price, which may differ from the stop price in fast-moving markets.

Usage Stop-Loss Orders: Traders use stop-loss orders primarily to manage risk and protect against significant losses in adverse market conditions. These conditions may include unexpected market movements, news events, or adverse price trends.

Advantages: The key advantage of stop-loss orders is their role in automatic risk management. They provide traders with a disciplined approach to limit losses, even in volatile market conditions. By setting stop-loss levels, traders can enforce risk control measures without constant monitoring of market movements.

Disadvantages: Despite their benefits, stop-loss orders are susceptible to slippage. Slippage occurs when the market moves quickly past the stop price, resulting in execution at a less favorable price than anticipated. This risk is particularly relevant in highly volatile markets or during periods of low liquidity.

4. COMBINING ORDER TYPES

Stop-Limit Orders: A stop-limit order combines features of both stop-loss and limit orders. Initially, it sets a stop price to trigger the order, similar to a stop-loss order. Once triggered, the order converts into a limit order, specifying the price at which the trade should be executed or better.

Usage: Traders use stop-limit orders to gain more control over the execution price while managing risk. For instance, setting a stop price at $50 and a limit price at $49 ensures that once the market reaches $50, the order will be executed at $49 or a better price. This strategy allows traders to avoid adverse price slippage while aiming to enter or exit positions at specific price levels.

Trailing Stop Orders: A trailing stop order is a type of stop-loss order that adjusts dynamically with the market price. It follows the asset's price direction, maintaining a specified distance, either in percentage or dollar terms. As the market price moves in favor of the trade, the trailing stop price automatically adjusts to lock in profits.

Usage: Traders commonly use trailing stop orders to secure profits while allowing for potential gains in volatile markets. For example, setting a trailing stop order at 5% below the market price means that if the price rises, the stop price will move up accordingly. If the price then falls by 5% from its highest point reached after the order is placed, the position will be sold, locking in profits without the need for constant monitoring.

PRACTICAL EXAMPLES OF USING ORDER TYPES

Market Order Example: A trader wants to buy 100 barrels of WTI crude oil immediately at the current market price. The trader places a market order, which is executed instantly at the best available price, ensuring immediate entry into the position.

Limit Order Example: A trader wants to buy 100 barrels of WTI crude oil but only if the price drops to $70 per barrel. The trader places a limit order at $70. The order will only be executed if the market price reaches $70 or lower, ensuring control over the entry price.

Stop-Loss Order Example: A trader holds a long position in Brent crude oil, bought at $75 per barrel, and wants to limit potential losses to $5 per barrel. The trader sets a stop-loss order at $70. If the price drops to $70, the order is triggered and executed as a market order, limiting the loss to $5 per barrel.

BEST PRACTICES FOR USING ORDER TYPES

Planning and Strategy: Integrate order types into the overall trading plan to ensure consistency and discipline. Set entry, exit, and stop-loss levels before entering trades to avoid emotional decision-making.

Monitoring and Adjusting: Monitor open orders and market conditions to make necessary adjustments. Be prepared to adjust orders based on changing market conditions, new information, or evolving trading strategies.

Risk Management: Always use stop-loss orders to manage risk and protect capital. Ensure that the size of each trade aligns with risk management rules and overall trading goals.

Understanding and effectively using different order types is crucial for successful oil trading. Market orders provide immediate execution, limit orders offer price control, and stop-loss orders protect against significant losses. By combining these order types and following best practices, traders can execute trades efficiently, manage risk, and achieve their trading goals.

Integrating order types into a comprehensive trading plan and continuously monitoring and adjusting orders based on market conditions will further enhance trading performance and long-term success.

CHAPTER 20: UNDERSTANDING SPREADS AND LEVERAGE

Spreads and leverage are two fundamental concepts that can significantly impact a trader's strategy and profitability. Spreads represent the difference between the buying and selling prices of an asset, playing a crucial role in determining trading costs. Leverage, on the other hand, involves borrowing funds to amplify trading positions, offering the potential for higher returns but also increasing the risk of substantial losses.

This chapter delves into the mechanics of spreads and leverage, providing a comprehensive understanding of how they function in various markets. By exploring different types of spreads and the implications of using leverage, traders can develop more informed and effective trading strategies.

INTRODUCTION TO SPREADS AND LEVERAGE

Spread: The difference between the bid (buy) and ask (sell) price of an asset. It represents the cost of trading.

Leverage: Leverage involves using borrowed funds to increase the potential return of an investment. By allowing traders to control larger positions with a smaller amount of capital, leverage can significantly amplify both gains and losses. It is a powerful tool in trading, providing the opportunity to maximize profits from market movements without requiring the full value of the trade upfront. However, it also introduces additional risk, as losses can exceed the initial investment, making effective leverage management crucial for long-term trading success.

Cost of Trading: Understanding spreads is crucial for evaluating the cost of entering and exiting positions, as it directly impacts the profitability of trades. Traders need to account for the spread to ensure their strategies are cost-effective and sustainable over the long term.

Risk and Reward: Leverage plays a significant role in magnifying both potential gains and potential losses. This dual-edged nature makes it imperative for traders to comprehend and manage leverage effectively. Proper use of leverage can enhance returns, but mismanagement can lead to substantial financial risk. Therefore, understanding these concepts is essential for making informed trading decisions and maintaining a balanced risk-reward ratio.

UNDERSTANDING SPREADS

1. Bid-Ask Spread

Bid Price: The highest price a buyer is willing to pay for an asset.

Ask Price: The lowest price a seller is willing to accept for an asset.

Spread Calculation: The spread is the difference between the ask and bid prices.

2. Types of Spreads

Fixed Spreads: Fixed Spreads refer to spreads that remain constant regardless of market conditions. They are typically offered in less volatile markets or by certain brokers who aim to provide consistent trading costs. This type of spread can offer traders predictability, making it easier to calculate trading costs and manage budgets.

Variable Spreads: Variable Spreads, on the other hand, fluctuate based on market conditions such as liquidity and volatility. These spreads are more common in highly traded markets like oil, where market dynamics can change rapidly. Variable spreads can widen during periods of high volatility or low liquidity, impacting trading costs. Traders need to be aware of these fluctuations and incorporate them into their trading strategies to manage costs effectively.

3. Factors Influencing Spreads

Liquidity: Liquidity plays a significant role in determining spreads. In markets with higher liquidity, where there are more buyers and sellers actively trading, spreads tend to be narrower. Conversely, in markets with lower liquidity, spreads are generally wider due to the decreased availability of matching buy and sell orders.

Volatility: Volatility is another crucial factor. During periods of increased market volatility, spreads can widen as market participants account for higher uncertainty and risk. This is especially relevant in highly traded commodities like oil, where price fluctuations can be significant.

Market Hours: Market Hours also affect spreads. Spreads can vary depending on the time of day and trading session. During off-peak times or when major markets are closed, spreads often widen due to reduced trading activity and liquidity.

4. Impact of Spreads on Trading

Cost Consideration: Cost Consideration is a vital aspect of trading, as spreads represent a direct cost that traders need to account for when calculating potential profits and losses. Understanding the impact of spreads helps traders better assess their true trading costs and adjust their strategies accordingly.

Frequent Trading: Frequent Trading can amplify the effect of spreads on overall performance. Traders who frequently enter and exit positions need to be mindful of the cumulative impact of spreads. Each trade incurs a cost due to the spread, and over time, these costs can add up, potentially affecting profitability. Properly accounting for spreads in trading plans and strategies is essential for maintaining a healthy trading balance.

UNDERSTANDING LEVERAGE

Leverage Ratio: The ratio of the trader's funds to the size of the position they can control. For example, a leverage ratio of 1:100 means a trader can control a position 100 times larger than their actual capital.

Leverage = Total Position Size / Trader's Capital.

Benefits of Leverage: Increased Buying Power is one of the primary benefits of leverage. By using borrowed funds, traders can take on larger positions than they could with their own capital alone. This amplifies the potential returns on successful trades, allowing traders to capitalize on market opportunities more effectively.

Capital Efficiency is another significant advantage. Leverage enables traders to use their capital more efficiently by freeing up funds that would otherwise be tied up in individual positions. This allows traders to diversify their investments across multiple positions or markets, potentially spreading risk and enhancing overall portfolio performance.

Risks of Leverage: Amplified Losses are a major risk associated with leverage. While leverage can increase potential profits, it also magnifies losses. Even a small adverse price movement can result in significant financial loss, potentially exceeding the initial investment.

Margin Calls are another critical risk. If the value of a leveraged position falls below a certain threshold, brokers may issue a margin call, requiring traders to deposit additional funds to maintain their positions. Failure to meet a margin call can result in the forced closure of positions, often at a loss.

Risk of Over-Leverage: The Risk of Over-Leverage involves the excessive use of borrowed funds, which can quickly deplete trading capital. Over-leveraging increases the likelihood of substantial losses and account liquidation, as traders may not have sufficient capital to cover adverse market movements.

PRACTICAL EXAMPLES OF SPREADS AND LEVERAGE

1. Spread Example: A trader is looking to buy 100 barrels of WTI crude oil. The bid price is $71.50, and the ask price is $72.00.

The spread is $72.00 - $71.50 = $0.50 per barrel. For 100 barrels, the total spread cost is $50.

2. Leverage Example: A trader has $1,000 in their account and uses 1:50 leverage to buy oil futures contracts worth $50,000.

A 1% increase in the price of oil results in a $500 profit (50% return on the trader's capital). Conversely, a 1% decrease results in a $500 loss.

MANAGING RISKS WITH SPREADS AND LEVERAGE

1. Spread Management: Effective Spread Management is crucial for optimizing trading costs and maximizing profitability: Opt for brokers offering competitive spreads. Lower spreads reduce the cost of entering and exiting positions, enhancing overall trading efficiency. Execute trades during periods of high liquidity and low volatility. These conditions typically result in narrower spreads, minimizing the cost of transactions.

2. Leverage Management: Sound Leverage Management is essential to mitigate risks and preserve trading capital. Familiarize yourself with the margin requirements set by brokers. Understand how leverage affects margin levels to avoid margin calls and potential liquidation.

Implement stop-loss orders to control risk. These orders help limit potential losses by automatically closing positions at predetermined levels, protecting against adverse market movements. Use leverage prudently based on your risk tolerance and trading experience. Avoid excessive leverage, which can amplify losses and potentially lead to account depletion or liquidation.

TOOLS AND RESOURCES FOR MANAGING SPREADS AND LEVERAGE

1. Trading Platforms: Utilizing advanced trading platforms enhances your ability to manage spreads and leverage effectively. Opt for platforms equipped with real-time spread data, leverage calculators, and integrated risk management tools. These features provide essential insights into market conditions and help in making informed trading decisions.

Customize trading settings to adjust leverage levels and establish predefined spread thresholds. Tailoring these settings allows you to align your trading strategy with risk tolerance and market conditions, optimizing performance.

2. Educational Resources: Continuous learning is essential for mastering spread and leverage management. Participate in webinars and structured courses offered by brokers and financial institutions. These educational sessions cover essential topics such as leverage dynamics and strategies for navigating varying spread conditions.

Supplement your knowledge with readings from reputable sources. Books and articles provide comprehensive insights into advanced techniques and real-world applications of spread and leverage management strategies.

3. Professional Advice: Seeking guidance from experienced professionals can significantly enhance your trading expertise. Engage with experienced traders or financial advisors who can provide personalized insights and strategies tailored to your trading goals. Their mentorship can help refine your approach to leverage utilization and spread management.

Trading Communities: Join trading communities and forums to participate in discussions and share experiences with peers. These platforms offer valuable networking opportunities and access to diverse perspectives on effective spread and leverage management strategies.

Comprehending the benefits and risks of leverage, using it judiciously, and implementing effective risk management strategies, helps traders maximize their potential while protecting their capital. Leveraging tools, resources, and professional advice further supports traders in navigating the complexities of spreads and leverage in the dynamic oil market.

CHAPTER 21: MANAGING OPEN POSITIONS

Managing open positions is a critical aspect of successful trading, requiring careful attention to market conditions, risk management, and strategic decision-making. Once a trade is initiated, effective management of open positions can determine the overall profitability and risk exposure of a trader's portfolio.

This chapter explores essential techniques and considerations for managing open positions, ranging from monitoring market movements and adjusting strategies to implementing risk management principles to safeguard capital.

INTRODUCTION TO POSITION MANAGEMENT

Position Management involves overseeing and adjusting open trading positions to achieve trading goals, manage risk, and maximize profits effectively. Effective position management serves two crucial purposes:

Risk Control: It helps traders mitigate risks and protect their capital by monitoring and adjusting positions based on market dynamics and risk tolerance.

Profit Optimization: Actively managing open positions allows traders to optimize profits by adapting strategies to changing market conditions and seizing profitable opportunities.

MONITORING OPEN POSITIONS

To effectively monitor open positions, traders should utilize:

Tools and Platforms: Utilize trading platforms equipped with real-time data, alerts, and notifications to stay informed about market movements affecting open positions.

Market News: Stay updated on relevant news and market events that could impact open positions, influencing trading decisions and risk management strategies.

Key Metrics to Track

When monitoring open positions, it's essential to track:

Price Movements: Monitor changes in asset prices to make timely decisions on whether to hold, adjust, or close positions based on market trends and analysis.

Position Size: Keep a close watch on the size of open positions relative to the overall portfolio, ensuring positions remain within predefined risk limits.

Profit and Loss (P&L): Continuously assess unrealized profits and losses associated with open positions to evaluate their performance and adjust strategies accordingly.

ADJUSTING STOP-LOSS AND TAKE-PROFIT LEVELS

1. Trailing Stop-Loss Orders

Trailing stop-loss orders are a dynamic risk management tool that adjusts automatically as the market price moves in favor of a trade.

Trailing stop-loss orders automatically adjust the stop-loss price as the market price moves in the trader's favor, thereby locking in profits or limiting losses.

Traders use trailing stop-loss orders primarily to protect profits. By setting a trailing stop-loss order at a specified distance from the current market price, traders can ensure that their profits are protected if the market reverses. This approach allows traders to capture potential gains while minimizing the risk of significant losses.

2. Moving Stop-Loss Orders

Moving stop-loss orders entail adjusting the stop-loss level manually as the market price moves in favor of the trade. This proactive approach aims to protect profits and minimize potential losses.

Strategy: Traders typically increase the stop-loss level incrementally as the market price advances in their favor. By doing so, traders aim to secure profits while allowing for potential further gains. This strategy helps in managing risk dynamically and adapting to changing market conditions.

3. Adjusting Take-Profit Levels

Strategy: Traders adjust take-profit levels based on current market conditions, new information, or changes in trading objectives. This strategic adaptation helps optimize trading outcomes and manage risk effectively.

Dynamic Targets: Setting dynamic take-profit targets involves adjusting profit objectives according to evolving market volatility and trends. This approach allows traders to capitalize on favorable price movements while mitigating potential losses during market fluctuations.

SCALING IN AND OUT OF POSITIONS

Scaling In: Scaling in refers to the strategy of gradually increasing the size of a position as the trade moves favorably for the trader. This approach allows traders to capitalize on momentum and maximize potential gains while managing risk effectively.

Traders implement scaling in by adding to winning positions in increments. This method helps to confirm the strength of the trade and can provide opportunities to adjust stop-loss levels to protect profits already gained. By scaling in, traders aim to optimize their entry points and overall position size relative to market movements.

Scaling Out: Scaling out involves gradually reducing the size of a position to secure profits while maintaining exposure to potential further gains in the market. It is a strategic approach to risk management and profit-taking.

Traders execute scaling out by selling portions of their position at predefined price levels. This method allows them to lock in profits as the market moves in their favor while still retaining a portion of the position to potentially benefit from continued price movement. Scaling out helps traders manage emotions and adhere to their trading plan by systematically realizing profits and reducing overall risk exposure over time.

HEDGING OPEN POSITIONS

Hedging refers to the practice of using financial instruments or market strategies to offset potential losses in an open position. Traders and investors hedge to protect themselves against adverse price movements in the assets they hold.

Hedging Strategies

Using Derivatives: One common hedging strategy involves the use of derivatives such as options, futures, or Contracts for Difference (CFDs). These instruments allow traders to establish positions that profit from price movements in the opposite direction of their existing positions, thereby mitigating potential losses.

Diversification: Another approach to hedging is through diversification. By spreading risk across multiple assets that may be correlated or uncorrelated, traders can reduce their exposure to specific market movements. Diversification is often used as a long-term risk management strategy across different asset classes and markets.

Example of Hedging

Suppose a trader holds a long position in Brent crude oil futures, anticipating a price increase due to geopolitical factors.

Execution: To hedge against the risk of a potential price drop in Brent crude oil, the trader decides to buy put options. Put options give the trader the right, but not the obligation, to sell Brent crude oil at a specified price (strike price) within a specific period. By purchasing put options, the trader can offset potential losses from the long position if the market price of Brent crude oil falls below the strike price of the options.

MANAGING EMOTIONS AND PSYCHOLOGY

1. Emotional Discipline

Control: Emotional discipline in trading involves adhering strictly to the trading plan and avoiding impulsive decisions driven by emotions such as fear or excitement. Traders maintain discipline by following predefined rules for entry, exit, and risk management, regardless of short-term market fluctuations.

Mindfulness: Practicing mindfulness techniques is crucial for maintaining composure and focus during volatile market conditions. Techniques such as meditation, deep breathing exercises, and mental visualization can help traders stay present and make rational decisions based on analysis rather than emotions.

2. Psychological Factors

Fear and Greed: Fear and greed are powerful emotions that can influence trading decisions. Fear of missing out (FOMO) may lead to chasing trades, while greed can cause traders to hold onto winning positions for too long. Recognizing these emotions and their potential impact allows traders to implement strategies to mitigate their influence, such as setting predefined entry and exit points.

Stress Management: Trading can be inherently stressful, especially during periods of market volatility. Effective stress management techniques are essential for maintaining mental and emotional well-being. Traders can reduce stress by taking regular breaks from trading, engaging in physical exercise, practicing relaxation techniques, and ensuring a balanced lifestyle outside of trading hours.

REVIEWING AND ANALYZING OPEN POSITIONS

1. Regular Reviews

Frequency: It's crucial to conduct frequent reviews of open positions to evaluate their performance and make necessary adjustments. Regular reviews allow traders to stay updated with market developments and ensure that positions align with current trading strategies and risk management rules.

Criteria: During these reviews, positions should be evaluated based on several factors, including prevailing market conditions, adherence to trading goals, and the effectiveness of risk management strategies. Assessing these criteria helps traders maintain a proactive approach to managing their portfolio.

2. Performance Analysis

Metrics: Analyzing key performance metrics provides valuable insights into the effectiveness of trading strategies. Metrics such as the win-loss ratio, average profit/loss per trade, and overall return on investment (ROI) help traders gauge their trading success and identify areas for improvement.

Lessons Learned: Reviewing both successful and unsuccessful trades allows traders to extract valuable lessons. Understanding what contributed to successful trades can help reinforce effective strategies, while analyzing mistakes from unsuccessful trades provides opportunities for learning and refinement. This continuous improvement process is essential for enhancing overall trading performance.

PRACTICAL EXAMPLE OF MANAGING OPEN POSITIONS

A trader initiates a long position by buying 200 barrels of WTI crude oil at $70 per barrel.

Stop-Loss and Take-Profit: The trader sets a stop-loss order at $65 to limit potential losses and a take-profit order at $80 to lock in profits.

Position Management

Monitoring: The trader regularly monitors price movements of WTI crude oil and stays updated with relevant market news that could impact the position.

Adjusting Stop-Loss: As the price of WTI crude oil rises to $75 per barrel, the trader adjusts the stop-loss order to $70 to lock in profits and protect against potential downside risk.

Scaling Out: With the price reaching $78 per barrel, the trader decides to sell 100 barrels of the position to secure partial profits while maintaining exposure to potential further gains with the remaining 100 barrels.

Hedging: To hedge against a potential price decline, the trader buys put options at $78 per barrel. This hedge allows them to protect the remaining 100 barrels of crude oil in case the market reverses.

Effective position management is crucial for successful oil trading. By monitoring open positions, adjusting stop-loss and take-profit levels, scaling in and out of positions, and employing hedging strategies, traders can manage risk and maximize profits. Maintaining emotional discipline and regularly reviewing and analyzing open positions further enhances trading performance.

Implementing these techniques within a comprehensive trading plan ensures that traders can navigate the complexities of the oil market with confidence and achieve long-term success.

PART 8: ADVANCED TRADING STRATEGIES

CHAPTER 22: SPREAD TRADING IN OIL MARKETS

In the world of commodities trading, spread trading plays a pivotal role in navigating the complexities of oil markets. Spread trading involves taking simultaneous positions in related assets, such as different oil futures contracts, to capitalize on price differentials and market dynamics. This chapter delves into the strategies, mechanics, and considerations involved in spread trading specifically within oil markets.

INTRODUCTION TO SPREAD TRADING

Spread trading is a sophisticated trading strategy that revolves around taking simultaneous long and short positions in two related financial instruments, aiming to profit from the price differential between them.

This strategy is commonly used in various financial markets, including commodities like oil, where different factors influence the pricing of related assets. Spread trading offers several strategic advantages that make it a preferred choice among traders:

Reduced Risk: By simultaneously holding long and short positions in related instruments, spread trading mitigates exposure to broader market movements. Instead of relying solely on the direction of a single asset, traders focus on the relative performance between two correlated assets.

Market Neutrality: One of the key benefits of spread trading is its ability to generate profit regardless of the overall market direction. This market-neutral approach allows traders to capitalize on price differentials between related assets, irrespective of whether the broader market is trending up, down, or sideways.

TYPES OF SPREADS IN OIL TRADING

1. Inter-Commodity Spreads

Inter-commodity spreads involve trading two different but related commodities. In the context of oil markets, traders often engage in spread trading between different types of crude oil, such as Brent crude oil and WTI (West Texas Intermediate) crude oil.

Example: Consider a trader who takes a long position in Brent crude oil futures and simultaneously takes a short position in WTI crude oil futures. The objective here is to profit from the price difference between these two crude oil benchmarks.

This type of spread trading allows traders to capitalize on the varying price differentials that exist due to factors such as regional supply and demand dynamics, transportation costs, and geopolitical influences affecting each type of crude oil.

2. Intra-Commodity Spreads

Intra-commodity spread trading involves trading futures contracts of the same commodity with different expiration dates. Traders use calendar spreads to capitalize on the price difference between contracts with varying maturity dates.

Example: A trader may initiate a calendar spread in WTI crude oil by going long on a near-term contract expiring in the current month, while simultaneously taking a short position on a further-term contract expiring in a subsequent month. By doing so, the trader aims to profit from the price discrepancy or convergence between these contracts as they approach expiration.

Location Spreads: Another form of intra-commodity spread trading involves trading the same commodity at different geographical locations.

Example: For instance, a trader might go long on Brent crude oil futures traded in Europe and simultaneously go short on Brent crude oil futures traded in the U.S. This strategy allows the trader to take advantage of price differentials influenced by regional supply and demand dynamics, transportation costs, and market conditions specific to each location.

3. Product Spreads

Crack Spreads: Product spread trading involves trading crude oil futures against its refined products, such as gasoline or heating oil. The term "crack" refers to the process of refining crude oil into these products.

Example: A trader could initiate a crack spread trade by taking a long position in crude oil futures while simultaneously taking a short position in gasoline futures. This strategy allows the trader to profit from the price difference, or spread, between crude oil and gasoline prices. The profitability of the crack spread is influenced by factors such as refining margins, supply and demand dynamics for crude oil and its products, and market conditions affecting energy markets.

KEY CONCEPTS IN SPREAD TRADING

Spread Ratio: The spread ratio refers to the proportion of quantities traded in the long and short positions to balance the spread trade effectively.

Calculation: It is calculated based on the relative values of the instruments involved in the spread. For example, if trading

Brent crude oil against WTI crude oil, the spread ratio would adjust according to their respective price movements to maintain balance in the trade.

Spread Width: Spread width is the absolute difference between the prices of the two instruments involved in a spread trade.

Importance: Understanding the spread width is crucial as it helps traders determine optimal entry and exit points for their trades. A wider spread may indicate greater potential profit but also higher risk, while a narrower spread may offer more conservative trading opportunities.

Spread Volatility: Spread volatility measures the degree of variation in the spread width over time.

Impact: Higher spread volatility signifies greater fluctuations in the price difference between the two instruments in the spread. While this volatility can potentially increase profits, it also introduces heightened risk due to the uncertainty in price movements. Traders often assess spread volatility to gauge potential profitability and manage risk accordingly in their spread trading strategies.

STRATEGIES FOR SPREAD TRADING

1. Calendar Spread Strategy

The calendar spread strategy involves analyzing seasonal patterns, supply-demand dynamics, and market expectations to identify profitable opportunities in futures contracts with different expiration dates.

Approach: Traders typically assess factors such as historical price movements during specific seasons, anticipated changes in supply and demand, and market sentiment regarding future price trends. For instance, during hurricane season, a trader might take a long position in near-term crude oil contracts and simultaneously short longer-term contracts to potentially profit from supply disruptions caused by adverse weather conditions.

Example: A trader anticipates increased volatility and potential supply disruptions in crude oil markets during hurricane season. They take a long position in September crude oil futures and a short position in December futures to capitalize on short-term price discrepancies caused by weather-related events.

2. Location Spread Strategy

The location spread strategy involves capitalizing on regional supply and demand differences, transportation costs, and geopolitical factors affecting the price of the same commodity traded in different locations.

Approach: Traders monitor factors such as regional production capabilities, infrastructure constraints, and geopolitical developments influencing supply chains. By analyzing these factors, traders aim to predict price differentials between different locations and capitalize on arbitrage opportunities.

Example: European demand for Brent crude oil increases due to temporary refinery outages affecting local supply. A trader decides to take a long position in Brent crude oil futures contracts traded in Europe while simultaneously shorting Brent crude oil futures contracts traded in the United States. This strategy allows the trader to profit from the anticipated price increase in Brent crude oil in Europe compared to the U.S. market.

3. Crack Spread Strategy

The crack spread strategy involves trading crude oil against its refined products, such as gasoline or heating oil, to profit from the price differential between the raw material and its derivatives.

Approach: Traders analyze refinery margins, inventory levels of crude oil and refined products, seasonal demand patterns, and market expectations for changes in fuel consumption. This strategy aims to capitalize on fluctuations in the price difference between crude oil and its refined products.

Example: During the summer driving season, demand for gasoline typically increases, affecting its price relative to crude oil. A trader takes a long position in crude oil futures contracts and simultaneously shorts gasoline futures contracts to profit from the expected widening of the crack spread. By doing so, the trader leverages the anticipated increase in gasoline prices relative to crude oil prices during peak demand periods.

TOOLS AND RESOURCES FOR SPREAD TRADING

1. Trading Platforms

When engaging in spread trading, selecting the right **trading platform** is crucial. Opt for platforms that offer robust features such as advanced charting, comprehensive analytics, and efficient execution capabilities tailored for spread trading strategies.

Examples: Platforms like Bloomberg Terminal and CME Group's trading platform are well-regarded for their extensive tools designed to support spread trading across various commodities, including crude oil.

2. Market Data and Analysis

Successful spread trading hinges on accurate and timely **market data and analysis**. Access to real-time and historical data on crude oil and related markets is essential for making informed decisions.

Data Sources: Utilize reputable data sources that provide comprehensive coverage of commodity markets, including price movements, volume trends, and market sentiment.

Analysis Tools: Employ sophisticated spread analysis tools available on trading platforms to identify potential trading opportunities and assess risk effectively. These tools often include comparative charting features and statistical analysis capabilities tailored for spread strategies.

3. Educational Resources

Continuous learning and staying updated with industry insights are vital for refining spread trading skills. Utilize a variety of **educational resources** to deepen your understanding of spread trading strategies and techniques.

Courses and Webinars: Enroll in courses and participate in webinars offered by reputable institutions and trading platforms. These educational sessions often cover advanced spread trading strategies, technical analysis methods, and market dynamics specific to commodities like crude oil.

Books and Articles: Expand your knowledge base by reading books authored by industry experts and articles that provide detailed case studies and practical insights into successful spread trading. These resources offer valuable perspectives on navigating volatile commodity markets and optimizing trading strategies.

MANAGING RISKS IN SPREAD TRADING

1. Risk Identification

Spread trading involves inherent risks that traders must identify and manage effectively:

Market Risk: This encompasses exposure to adverse price movements in the underlying instruments involved in the spread trade, such as crude oil futures or options.

Liquidity Risk: Traders may encounter challenges in entering or exiting spread positions due to low market liquidity, which can affect trade execution and pricing.

Execution Risk: There is a risk of slippage or delays in executing spread trades at desired prices, especially in volatile market conditions.

2. Risk Mitigation

To mitigate the risks associated with spread trading, traders employ several strategies:

Diversification: Spread risk across multiple spread trades and different instruments to reduce reliance on a single position or market.

Position Sizing: Use appropriate position sizing techniques to manage potential losses relative to overall trading capital and risk tolerance.

Stop-Loss Orders: Implement stop-loss orders to automatically exit spread positions if the market moves unfavorably beyond a predefined point. This helps limit potential losses and protect trading capital.

3. Continuous Monitoring

Successful spread trading requires continuous monitoring and adjustment:

Market Conditions: Regularly review market conditions, including changes in supply-demand dynamics, economic indicators, and geopolitical events that may impact spread trades.

Performance Metrics: Track key performance metrics such as changes in spread width, profit and loss (P&L), and risk-adjusted returns. This analysis provides insights into the effectiveness of spread trading strategies and helps in making informed decisions.

Spread trading in oil markets offers a way to profit from relative price movements while reducing exposure to overall market volatility. By understanding different types of spreads, key concepts, and strategies, traders can effectively manage risk and optimize returns.

Utilizing advanced trading platforms, market data, and educational resources further enhances the ability to identify and execute profitable spread trades. With continuous monitoring and risk management, spread trading can be a valuable addition to a trader's arsenal in navigating the complexities of the oil market.

CHAPTER 23: HEDGING WITH FUTURES AND OPTIONS

Hedging is a fundamental risk management strategy used by traders and businesses to mitigate the impact of adverse price movements in financial markets. In the context of commodities like crude oil, where price volatility can significantly affect profitability, hedging plays a crucial role in stabilizing revenues and protecting against potential losses.

This chapter explores how futures and options contracts are utilized as hedging instruments in commodity markets, with a specific focus on crude oil. It delves into the mechanics of hedging, the strategic use of derivatives to offset price risk, and practical examples of how futures and options can be employed to manage exposure effectively.

INTRODUCTION TO HEDGING

Hedging is a risk management strategy used to offset potential losses from adverse price movements in the underlying asset. In the context of commodities like crude oil, where price volatility can lead to substantial financial exposure, hedging allows market participants to mitigate these risks by taking positions that counterbalance their existing market positions. Hedging plays a crucial role in risk mitigation within commodity markets:

Risk Mitigation: By hedging, traders and investors can protect themselves against price volatility and the potential for unexpected market fluctuations. This ensures that adverse price movements in the underlying asset do not result in significant financial losses.

Stabilizing Cash Flows: For producers, consumers, and investors alike, hedging ensures more predictable revenues and costs. This stability is essential for planning and budgeting, especially in industries heavily influenced by commodity price movements.

HEDGING INSTRUMENTS IN OIL MARKETS

1. Futures Contracts

Futures contracts are standardized agreements to buy or sell a specified amount of crude oil at a predetermined price and date in the future. These contracts facilitate hedging by allowing market participants to lock in prices today for future delivery, thereby managing price risk effectively.

Usage: Producers and consumers of crude oil frequently utilize futures contracts to hedge against price fluctuations. For instance, a producer can lock in a future selling price through a futures contract, protecting against potential declines in the market price of crude oil. Similarly, consumers can secure future purchasing costs, ensuring stability in their supply chain and budgeting processes.

2. Options Contracts

Options contracts provide the holder with the right, but not the obligation, to buy (call option) or sell (put option) a specified amount of crude oil at a predetermined price (strike price) within a specified period. Unlike futures contracts, options offer flexibility in hedging strategies by providing the potential to benefit from favorable price movements while limiting downside risk.

Usage: Options are used strategically in hedging to manage risk exposure while maintaining the opportunity for gains. For instance, a producer expecting future price volatility might purchase put options to protect against price declines, while still benefiting from potential price increases through the underlying physical position.

TYPES OF HEDGING STRATEGIES

1. Futures Hedging

Scenario: An oil producer anticipates delivering crude oil in three months and wants to secure the selling price amid market uncertainty.

Strategy: The producer decides to hedge against potential price declines by selling futures contracts. By selling futures contracts, the producer locks in the current price for crude oil delivery in three months. This strategy effectively mitigates the risk of falling oil prices, ensuring a predictable revenue stream from the future sale of crude oil.

2. Options Hedging

Scenario: An airline company foresees geopolitical tensions that could lead to higher jet fuel prices in the coming months.

Strategy: To protect against potential price increases, the airline opts to hedge using call options. By purchasing call options, the airline gains the right (but not the obligation) to buy jet fuel at a predetermined price within a specified period. This strategy allows the airline to limit its exposure to higher fuel costs while retaining the flexibility to benefit from any favorable price movements in the underlying jet fuel market.

PRACTICAL EXAMPLES OF HEDGING

1. FUTURES HEDGING EXAMPLE

Scenario: An oil producer plans to produce 10,000 barrels of crude oil in six months and is concerned about potential price fluctuations affecting revenue.

Execution: To hedge against the risk of falling oil prices, the producer decides to sell 10 futures contracts. Each futures contract represents the obligation to deliver 1,000 barrels of crude oil at a predetermined price (the futures price) on a specified future date. By selling futures contracts, the producer locks in the current market price for the future delivery of crude oil. This hedging strategy ensures that regardless of price movements in the market over the next six months, the producer will receive the agreed-upon price for the 10,000 barrels of crude oil produced.

2. OPTIONS HEDGING EXAMPLE

Scenario: An investor holds refinery stocks and is concerned about potential declines in oil prices, which could adversely affect the profitability of refinery operations.

Execution: To protect against the downside risk of falling oil prices, the investor purchases put options. A put option gives the holder the right (but not the obligation) to sell a specified amount of crude oil (or its equivalent in futures contracts) at a predetermined price (the strike price) within a specified period (until the option expiration date). By purchasing put options, the investor can profit if the price of crude oil declines below the strike price. This hedging strategy helps mitigate potential losses in the value of refinery stocks due to adverse movements in oil prices, while allowing the investor to benefit from any gains in the put options if oil prices decrease.

BENEFITS OF HEDGING

1. PRICE CERTAINTY

Futures: Futures contracts enable participants to lock in prices for future transactions, thereby protecting against adverse price movements. For example, an oil producer can sell futures contracts to secure a predetermined selling price for their oil production, ensuring price certainty even if market prices decline.

Options: Options contracts offer flexibility while providing protection against downside risk. By purchasing put options, for instance, market participants can safeguard against potential losses if oil prices fall below a specified strike price. Unlike futures, options provide the right but not the obligation to execute the contract, allowing holders to benefit from favorable price movements while limiting downside risk.

2. RISK MANAGEMENT

Financial Stability: Hedging with futures and options ensures predictable costs and revenues, enhancing financial stability for businesses involved in oil production, refining, or consumption. Producers and consumers alike utilize these financial instruments to manage the impact of volatile oil prices on their operations, maintaining stability in cash flows and budget planning.

Portfolio Protection: Investors can use futures and options to mitigate losses in investment portfolios exposed to oil price fluctuations. For instance, purchasing put options on oil-related stocks can act as insurance against declines in their market value due to falling oil prices. This hedging strategy helps investors safeguard their portfolios while potentially benefiting from other market opportunities.

CHALLENGES OF HEDGING

1. BASIS RISK

Basis risk refers to the risk that the price movements of the hedge instrument (such as futures or options) may not perfectly correlate with those of the underlying asset (like crude oil). This discrepancy can result in imperfect hedging outcomes, leading to potential losses or reduced effectiveness of the hedge.

Management: To manage basis risk effectively, market participants actively monitor and adjust their hedging strategies. This involves regularly assessing the relationship between the hedge instrument and the underlying asset. Adjustments may include revising the size or timing of the hedge, switching to different contract months in futures trading, or considering alternative strike prices in options trading.

By actively managing basis risk, participants aim to align their hedge positions more closely with their exposure to the underlying asset, thereby enhancing the effectiveness of their risk management strategy.

2. COST CONSIDERATIONS

Futures: When using futures contracts for hedging, market participants must consider initial margin requirements and potential margin calls. Initial margin represents the amount of capital required to initiate a futures position, which acts as a security deposit. Margin calls may occur if the value of the futures position declines, requiring additional funds to maintain the required margin level. These costs are important considerations in managing futures positions and ensuring adequate liquidity to meet margin obligations.

Options: Options contracts involve premium costs paid upfront by the buyer to acquire the right, but not the obligation, to buy (call option) or sell (put option) the underlying asset at a predetermined price within a specified period. The premium cost represents the price of the option and is determined by factors such as the volatility of the underlying asset, the time until expiration, and the strike price. Market participants assess these premium costs carefully when hedging with options, weighing the benefits of downside protection against the initial expense incurred.

STRATEGIES FOR EFFECTIVE HEDGING

1. TIMING OF HEDGING

Forward Planning: Effective hedging strategies often involve planning and executing hedge positions well in advance of anticipated market movements. This proactive approach allows market participants to secure favorable prices and protect against adverse price fluctuations in the underlying asset, such as crude oil. By hedging early, businesses can stabilize costs or revenues associated with future transactions, thereby enhancing financial predictability and reducing uncertainty.

Market Analysis: Utilizing both technical and fundamental analysis plays a crucial role in determining the timing of hedging activities. Technical analysis involves studying historical price patterns and market trends to identify opportune moments for entering hedge positions. Fundamental analysis, on the other hand, examines broader economic factors, supply-demand dynamics, geopolitical events, and market sentiment to gauge future price movements. By combining these analytical approaches, market participants can make informed decisions on when to initiate hedging strategies, optimizing their risk management efforts.

2. DIVERSIFICATION

Portfolio Approach: Diversification in hedging involves spreading risk across different time periods and financial instruments within the crude oil market. This approach mitigates the impact of adverse price movements on the overall portfolio. For example, a company may hedge its exposure to crude oil price volatility by employing futures contracts with varying expiration dates. By diversifying across multiple contract months, businesses reduce the risk of losses from concentrated positions in any single futures contract, enhancing portfolio resilience.

Asset Allocation: Balancing hedged and unhedged positions based on prevailing market conditions is essential for effective risk management. Market participants adjust their asset allocation between hedged and unhedged positions in response to changes in price volatility, market liquidity, and risk appetite. During periods of heightened uncertainty or anticipated price fluctuations in crude oil markets, increasing hedge positions may provide greater stability and downside protection. Conversely, adjusting towards unhedged positions during stable market conditions allows participants to capitalize on potential market opportunities and optimize returns.

TOOLS AND RESOURCES FOR HEDGING

1. Hedging Platforms

Features: Hedging platforms play a crucial role in facilitating effective risk management strategies in commodities like crude oil. These platforms offer market participants access to futures and options markets, providing essential tools and functionalities to execute and manage hedging positions effectively. Key features include:

Access to Markets: Platforms such as CME Group and ICE Futures provide access to a wide range of futures and options contracts, allowing participants to hedge against price fluctuations in crude oil and other commodities.

Risk Management Tools: Robust risk management tools are integrated into these platforms, enabling users to monitor market trends, analyze price movements, and implement hedging strategies based on real-time data and market insights.

Examples:

CME Group: Known for its extensive offerings in energy futures and options, CME Group provides liquidity and transparency in global markets, essential for hedging strategies in crude oil.

ICE Futures: Offers futures and options contracts across various commodities, including energy products like crude oil, providing hedging solutions tailored to market participants' needs.

2. Risk Management Tools

Analytical Software: Advanced analytical software plays a pivotal role in enhancing risk management capabilities within the crude oil hedging context. These tools enable market participants to conduct scenario analysis, stress testing, and sensitivity analysis to assess potential impacts on hedging positions. Key functionalities include:

Scenario Analysis: Allows users to simulate various market scenarios to evaluate the effectiveness of hedging strategies under different conditions, such as price volatility or supply disruptions.

Stress Testing: Assesses the resilience of hedging portfolios by subjecting them to extreme market conditions or adverse events, identifying potential vulnerabilities and optimizing risk mitigation strategies.

Sensitivity Analysis: Measures the sensitivity of hedging positions to changes in key variables, such as crude oil prices, interest rates, or geopolitical factors, helping participants refine their hedging strategies based on risk exposure.

Educational Resources: Comprehensive educational resources are essential for market participants to enhance their understanding of hedging strategies and best practices. These resources include:

Courses and Webinars: Offered by hedging platforms, financial institutions, and industry experts, these educational sessions provide insights into effective hedging techniques, market trends, and regulatory developments.

Publications: Access to research papers, industry reports, and publications that offer in-depth analysis of crude oil markets, hedging strategies, and case studies, helping participants stay informed and make informed decisions.

Hedging with futures and options is a powerful risk management tool in the volatile oil markets. By utilizing futures contracts to lock in prices and options contracts to protect against adverse price movements, market participants can stabilize cash flows and protect profitability.

Understanding different hedging strategies, their benefits, and challenges is essential for effective risk management and financial stability. With access to advanced hedging platforms, analytical tools, and educational resources, traders and businesses can navigate the complexities of hedging in oil markets with confidence and achieve long-term success.

CHAPTER 24: SWING TRADING AND DAY TRADING TECHNIQUES

Swing trading and day trading stand out as popular strategies among active traders seeking to capitalize on short-term price movements. These techniques are distinct in their approaches and time horizons, yet both share a common goal: to profit from market fluctuations over relatively brief periods. While swing trading focuses on capturing larger price movements over days to weeks, day trading involves executing trades within the same trading day to exploit intraday price fluctuations.

This chapter explores the principles, strategies, and tools essential for successful swing trading and day trading. From mastering technical indicators to implementing risk management practices, each section provides insights tailored to navigate the complexities of these fast-paced trading environments.

INTRODUCTION TO SWING TRADING AND DAY TRADING

Swing Trading: Swing trading is a trading strategy focused on capturing short- to medium-term gains in a financial instrument over a period ranging from several days to weeks. It typically relies on technical analysis to identify opportunities based on price momentum and chart patterns.

Day Trading: Day trading involves the buying and selling of financial instruments within the same trading day to profit from intraday price movements. Day traders capitalize on volatility and short-term price fluctuations, aiming to exploit market inefficiencies throughout the trading session.

Profit Potential: Both swing trading and day trading present opportunities for traders to capitalize on short-term price movements and generate profits. Swing traders seek to capture larger price swings over a defined period, while day traders focus on rapid, intraday price changes.

Flexibility: These trading techniques offer flexibility to adapt to different market conditions and trader preferences. Swing trading accommodates traders looking for less frequent trades with potentially larger gains, while day trading appeals to those seeking quick, frequent trading opportunities.

TECHNIQUES FOR SWING TRADING

1. Technical Analysis

Technical analysis forms the backbone of both swing trading and day trading strategies, leveraging historical price data and market activity to forecast future price movements.

Chart Patterns: Utilize patterns such as head and shoulders, triangles, and double tops/bottoms to identify potential trend reversals or continuations.

Indicators: Incorporate technical indicators like moving averages, MACD (Moving Average Convergence Divergence), RSI (Relative Strength Index), and Fibonacci retracements to generate entry and exit signals based on price momentum and market trends.

2. Fundamental Analysis

While less emphasized in day trading, fundamental analysis plays a crucial role in swing trading by evaluating broader market conditions and economic factors influencing price movements.

Market News: Stay informed about economic data releases, geopolitical events, and industry-specific news that can impact market sentiment and asset prices.

Sector Analysis: Focus on specific sectors or industries experiencing growth or regulatory changes, identifying opportunities for swing trades based on fundamental shifts.

3. Risk Management

Effective risk management is essential for both swing trading and day trading strategies, ensuring capital preservation and sustainable trading performance.

Stop-Loss Orders: Implement stop-loss orders to establish predefined exit points that protect against significant losses in volatile market conditions.

Position Sizing: Manage risk by determining appropriate position sizes relative to account size and risk tolerance, typically allocating a small percentage of capital per trade.

Profit Targets: Set profit-taking levels based on technical indicators, chart patterns, or fundamental analysis to capture gains while maintaining disciplined trading practices.

TECHNIQUES FOR DAY TRADING

1. Technical Analysis

In day trading, technical analysis plays a pivotal role in making rapid trading decisions based on real-time market data.

Intraday Charts: Utilize shorter timeframes such as 1-minute or 5-minute charts to capture quick price movements and identify intraday trends effectively.

Volume and Liquidity: Focus on trading in highly liquid markets with substantial trading volume to ensure efficient order execution and minimal slippage.

2. Scalping and Momentum Trading

Day trading involves two prominent strategies: scalping and momentum trading, each leveraging short-term price movements for profit.

Scalping: Execute numerous trades throughout the day to profit from small price fluctuations, aiming for incremental gains on each trade with tight stop-loss orders.

Momentum Trading: Capitalize on strong price moves driven by market momentum, entering trades swiftly to ride the trend and exiting before momentum shifts.

3. News and Catalysts

Market-moving events and news releases are critical for day traders, influencing short-term price movements and trading opportunities.

Market Open: React to pre-market and early morning news releases that impact stock prices, taking advantage of initial volatility and trading opportunities.

Earnings Reports: Trade around quarterly earnings announcements, capitalizing on heightened volatility and rapid price movements driven by earnings surprises or disappointments.

TOOLS AND RESOURCES FOR SWING TRADING AND DAY TRADING

1. Trading Platforms

For both swing trading and day trading, selecting the right platform is crucial for accessing real-time data, executing trades swiftly, and utilizing advanced charting tools.

Features: Opt for platforms that offer comprehensive features such as real-time market data, customizable charts with technical indicators, and efficient order execution capabilities suitable for rapid trading decisions.

Examples: Consider popular platforms like MetaTrader, Thinkorswim by TD Ameritrade, and Interactive Brokers for their robust functionalities tailored to both swing and day trading needs.

2. Technical Analysis Tools

Technical analysis forms the backbone of trading strategies, enabling traders to identify potential opportunities and make informed decisions.

Screeners: Use stock screeners and scanners to filter stocks based on predefined criteria such as price movements, volume, and technical indicators, facilitating the identification of potential trades.

Algorithmic Trading: Explore algorithmic trading strategies that automate trade execution based on predefined technical signals and market patterns, enhancing efficiency and reducing emotional biases.

3. Risk Management Tools

Effective risk management is essential in minimizing potential losses and preserving capital in both swing trading and day trading environments.

Simulation Platforms: Practice trading strategies in simulated environments offered by platforms like paper trading or demo accounts, allowing traders to hone their skills and test new strategies without financial risk.

Educational Resources: Stay informed and continuously learn through webinars, books, and participation in trading communities that provide insights into advanced risk management techniques and current market trends.

PSYCHOLOGICAL CONSIDERATIONS

Successful swing trading and day trading require strong psychological discipline and effective stress management techniques.

1. Discipline and Patience

Maintaining discipline and patience is crucial to staying focused and executing trading strategies effectively:

Stick to Trading Plan: Adhere to predefined trading rules, including entry and exit points, to minimize emotional decision-making and maintain consistency in trading performance.

Emotional Control: Manage emotions such as fear and greed by remaining objective and detached from individual trades. Emphasize rational decision-making based on analysis rather than emotional impulses.

2. Stress Management

Effective stress management enhances trading performance and decision-making capabilities:

Healthy Habits: Adopt a balanced lifestyle that includes regular exercise, sufficient sleep, and stress-relief techniques like meditation or hobbies. These practices help in reducing stress levels and maintaining mental clarity during trading hours.

ADVANTAGES AND CHALLENGES

1. Advantages

Swing trading and day trading offer distinct advantages for traders seeking short-term opportunities in the market:

Profit Potential: Both strategies enable traders to capitalize on short-term price movements, potentially generating quick profits based on market volatility and momentum.

Flexibility: Traders can adapt their strategies to various market conditions, choosing trading styles that align with their preferences and risk tolerance levels.

2. Challenges

Despite their advantages, swing trading and day trading present challenges that traders must navigate:

Time Commitment: Active trading requires continuous monitoring of price movements and market news throughout the trading session, demanding significant time and attention from traders.

Risk Management: Managing volatility and market risks is crucial in short-term trading, as rapid price fluctuations can lead to substantial losses if risk management strategies are not implemented effectively.

Swing trading and day trading are dynamic strategies suited for traders seeking to profit from short-term market fluctuations in oil and other financial markets. By mastering technical and fundamental analysis techniques, implementing effective risk management strategies, and leveraging advanced trading tools, traders can enhance their ability to identify and capitalize on trading opportunities.

Understanding the psychological aspects and maintaining discipline are crucial for success in swing trading and day trading. With continuous learning, practice, and adaptation to market conditions, traders can navigate the complexities of short-term trading and achieve their financial goals.

PART 9: RISK MANAGEMENT AND PSYCHOLOGY

CHAPTER 25: IDENTIFYING AND MITIGATING RISKS

Trading in the financial markets inherently involves risk, and managing that risk is a critical component of successful trading. Whether you're trading crude oil, equities, or any other financial instrument, understanding the types of risks you face and implementing effective risk mitigation strategies is essential.

This chapter delves into the various risks associated with trading and provides practical approaches to manage and mitigate these risks, ensuring that traders are well-prepared to handle adverse market conditions.

INTRODUCTION TO RISK MANAGEMENT

The process of identifying, assessing, and controlling potential risks to minimize their impact on trading and investment activities.

Preservation of Capital: Protecting capital from losses due to market volatility and unforeseen events is crucial for long-term trading success. Effective risk management ensures that traders can withstand adverse market conditions without suffering devastating financial losses.

Enhanced Decision-Making: Making informed decisions based on risk assessment and mitigation strategies allows traders to approach the market with a clear plan and confidence. This reduces the likelihood of emotional or impulsive trading decisions.

TYPES OF RISKS IN OIL TRADING

1. MARKET RISK

Market risk is the potential for financial loss due to adverse price movements in the oil market. This risk arises from the inherent volatility of oil prices, influenced by various factors such as geopolitical events, economic conditions, and changes in supply and demand. Market risk affects both short-term traders and long-term investors, as fluctuations in oil prices can lead to significant gains or losses in their positions.

Examples:

Price Volatility: Sudden and significant changes in oil prices can result from various factors, including economic reports, changes in global demand, and speculative trading. These price swings can lead to unexpected losses or gains.

Geopolitical Events: Political instability, wars, and decisions by major oil-producing nations (such as OPEC decisions) can drastically affect oil supply and prices. For example, conflicts in the Middle East often lead to fears of supply disruptions, causing price spikes.

Supply-Demand Imbalances: Situations where supply exceeds demand or vice versa can cause price fluctuations. For example, an oversupply due to increased shale production or a sudden drop in demand due to a global economic slowdown can lead to significant price movements.

2. CREDIT RISK

Credit risk is the potential for financial loss arising from the failure of a counterparty to meet its contractual obligations. This can occur if the counterparty defaults on a loan, fails to make a required payment, or is unable to fulfill the terms of a financial agreement.

In the context of trading, credit risk can affect transactions involving brokers, derivatives, and other financial instruments, where the solvency and reliability of the counterparty are crucial for the completion and settlement of trades.

Examples:

Brokerage Defaults: If a brokerage firm goes bankrupt or faces financial difficulties, clients may lose access to their funds or face significant delays in accessing their capital.

Counterparty Failure in Derivatives Transactions: In derivative contracts such as futures or options, if the counterparty defaults, the trader may not receive the promised payout, leading to financial loss. For example, during the financial crisis of 2008, many counterparties failed to meet their obligations, leading to substantial losses.

3. OPERATIONAL RISK

Operational risk refers to the potential for loss resulting from inadequate or failed internal processes, systems, or human error. This type of risk encompasses a wide range of issues that can disrupt or negatively impact the normal functioning of operations within an organization or trading environment.

Examples:

Trading Errors: Mistakes made during the execution of trades, such as entering the wrong order size or price, can result in unintended positions and significant financial losses.

Technological Failures: Downtime or malfunctions of trading platforms, data feeds, or other critical systems can disrupt trading activities. For instance, if a trader cannot execute a trade due to a platform crash, they might miss profitable opportunities or fail to exit losing positions.

Compliance Breaches: Violations of regulatory requirements or internal policies can lead to legal penalties, fines, and reputational damage. For example, failing to adhere to anti-money laundering (AML) regulations can result in severe fines from regulatory bodies.

4. LIQUIDITY RISK

Liquidity risk refers to the potential difficulty or inability to buy or sell assets at desired prices or volumes due to insufficient market liquidity. Liquidity risk arises when trading volumes are low, bid-ask spreads widen, or market depth is insufficient to accommodate large transactions without impacting prices adversely.

Examples:

Thinly Traded Instruments: Securities or contracts with low trading volume can be challenging to buy or sell without significantly impacting the price. For example, certain oil futures contracts might not have enough buyers or sellers, making it hard to enter or exit positions at desired prices.

Market Disruptions: Events such as market crashes, extreme volatility, or sudden regulatory changes can disrupt normal trading activities, leading to a lack of liquidity. For instance, during the 2020 COVID-19 pandemic, many markets experienced extreme volatility, making it difficult for traders to execute orders without large price concessions.

5. REGULATORY RISK

Regulatory risk refers to the potential for adverse impacts on trading activities or investments due to changes in regulations or government policies. These changes can affect various aspects of market operations, including trading practices, compliance requirements, tax policies, and market access rules. Regulatory risk arises from uncertainties about how new regulations will be implemented and their potential effects on market participants.

Examples:

New Tax Policies: Implementation of new taxes on trading profits or transactions can affect profitability. For example, a financial transaction tax (FTT) imposed on each trade can reduce overall returns.

Regulatory Bans or Restrictions: Introduction of new rules that restrict or ban certain trading practices or instruments can limit trading opportunities and strategies. For instance, a ban on certain types of speculative trading or tighter regulations on derivatives could impact the ability to hedge or speculate effectively.

RISK IDENTIFICATION AND ASSESSMENT

1. RISK IDENTIFICATION

Risk identification involves systematically identifying potential risks that could impact oil trading activities. This includes analyzing market conditions (such as price volatility and geopolitical events), assessing operational processes (like trading execution and risk management protocols), and evaluating external factors (such as regulatory changes and economic trends).

Tools: Traders and firms utilize several tools to identify risks effectively:

Risk Registers: Structured databases or systems that catalog identified risks along with their characteristics and potential impacts.

Scenario Analysis: Creating hypothetical scenarios to assess how different risk events could unfold and their implications.

Historical Data: Reviewing past market behaviors and events to identify recurring patterns or potential risk triggers.

2. RISK ASSESSMENT

Quantitative Analysis:

Assessing risks quantitatively involves using statistical models and data to measure the probability of occurrence and potential financial impact. This includes:

Probability Assessment: Estimating the likelihood of each identified risk event occurring based on historical data or market intelligence.

Impact Analysis: Evaluating the potential financial consequences of each risk event on trading positions, portfolios, and overall financial performance.

Qualitative Analysis:

In addition to quantitative metrics, qualitative factors are also considered:

Market Sentiment: Assessing market participants' perceptions, attitudes, and behavioral trends that could influence risk dynamics.

Regulatory Changes: Considering the impact of new or changing regulations on trading strategies and compliance requirements.

RISK MITIGATION STRATEGIES

1. Diversification

Portfolio Diversification: Spread investments across different asset classes, sectors, and geographical regions to reduce concentration risk. In oil trading, this could involve diversifying across various energy commodities (crude oil, natural gas), different oil-producing regions, and related sectors such as energy infrastructure and renewable energy.

Instrument Diversification: Trade a variety of oil derivatives to hedge against specific market risks. This includes using futures contracts for direct exposure to oil price movements and options contracts for more flexible risk management strategies, such as hedging against downside risk while allowing for potential upside gains.

2. Hedging

Futures and Options: Utilize derivatives like futures and options to offset price fluctuations and manage exposure to market risk. Oil producers, consumers, and traders can use futures contracts to lock in prices for future delivery of crude oil, thereby mitigating the risk of adverse price movements. Options provide the right (but not the obligation) to buy or sell oil at a predetermined price, offering flexibility in managing risk.

Strategies: Employ futures contracts for price hedging, enabling parties to secure a known price for future transactions. Options can be used to protect against downside risk (using put options) or capitalize on potential price increases (using call options), depending on market conditions and trading objectives.

3. Stop-Loss Orders

Implement predefined orders to automatically sell an asset if it reaches a specified price level, thereby limiting potential losses. In oil trading, stop-loss orders are crucial for managing risk and protecting capital against sudden price movements.

Implementation: Determine stop-loss levels based on technical analysis indicators (such as support and resistance levels), individual risk tolerance, and specific trading strategies. Adjust stop-loss orders as market conditions change to optimize risk management.

4. Position Sizing

Calculate the amount of capital allocated to each trade based on risk appetite, portfolio size, and risk assessment. Proper position sizing ensures that no single trade significantly impacts overall portfolio performance.

Risk-Reward Ratio: Maintain a favorable risk-reward ratio by assessing potential gains relative to potential losses for each trade. This ratio helps traders evaluate whether a trade is worth pursuing based on the expected return compared to the risk taken.

ADVANCED RISK MANAGEMENT TECHNIQUES

1. Stress Testing

Evaluate portfolio performance under extreme market conditions to assess resilience and identify vulnerabilities. Stress testing involves simulating adverse scenarios to understand potential losses and liquidity needs during crises.

Scenario Analysis: Model potential outcomes based on different economic scenarios and market events. By analyzing how portfolios would react to various shocks (e.g., oil price crashes, geopolitical disruptions), traders can better prepare and adjust risk management strategies accordingly.

2. Algorithmic Risk Management

Automated Systems: Use algorithms and trading software to monitor risks in real time and execute predefined risk management rules. Algorithmic trading systems can swiftly respond to market movements, execute trades, and adjust positions based on predefined risk parameters.

AI and Machine Learning: Employ advanced analytics to predict market movements and optimize risk-adjusted returns. Machine learning algorithms analyze large datasets to identify patterns and anomalies, enhancing decision-making in risk management.

COMPLIANCE AND REGULATORY CONSIDERATIONS

Regulatory Compliance

Adherence: Comply with financial regulations, reporting requirements, and trading restrictions applicable to oil trading activities. Regulatory compliance ensures adherence to laws governing financial markets, protecting traders and investors from legal and financial risks.

Documentation: Maintain accurate records of transactions, risk assessments, and compliance measures. Detailed documentation facilitates transparency, audit trails, and regulatory reporting, essential for demonstrating regulatory compliance.

PSYCHOLOGICAL ASPECTS OF RISK MANAGEMENT

Emotion Control

Discipline: Avoid emotional trading decisions by adhering to predefined risk management strategies. Emotional discipline helps traders maintain rational decision-making, reducing the impact of fear and greed on trading outcomes.

Mindfulness: Practice mindfulness techniques to stay focused and objective during periods of market volatility. Mindfulness enhances awareness of one's emotions and thought processes, fostering better stress management and decision-making under pressure.

CONTINUOUS MONITORING AND EVALUATION

Monitoring Risks

Real-Time Monitoring: Use trading platforms and analytics tools to monitor market conditions and portfolio performance. Real-time data and analytics enable proactive risk management, allowing traders to react swiftly to changing market dynamics.

Periodic Reviews: Conduct regular reviews of risk management strategies and adjust them based on evolving market conditions. Periodic evaluations ensure that risk management practices remain effective and aligned with trading objectives, incorporating lessons learned from past experiences.

Effective risk management is essential for navigating the complexities of oil trading and ensuring long-term profitability and capital preservation. By identifying, assessing, and mitigating various types of risks—from market volatility and operational failures to regulatory changes—traders can optimize their trading strategies and enhance decision-making processes.

CHAPTER 26: DEALING WITH MARKET VOLATILITY

Market volatility is an inherent characteristic of financial markets, reflecting the rapid and often unpredictable changes in asset prices. In the oil market, volatility can be driven by various factors, including geopolitical events, changes in supply and demand dynamics, economic data releases, and natural disasters.

UNDERSTANDING MARKET VOLATILITY

Market Volatility is the degree of variation in the price of a financial instrument over time, reflecting uncertainty and risk in the market. It is often measured by the standard deviation or variance of returns and can indicate the level of risk associated with the asset.

Impact on Trading: Market volatility significantly influences trading decisions, risk management strategies, and overall portfolio performance. High volatility can lead to rapid price movements, creating both opportunities and challenges for traders.

Opportunity and Risk: While volatility provides opportunities for profit by capitalizing on price swings, it also increases the risk of losses. Effective risk management strategies are essential to navigate the uncertainties presented by volatile markets.

CAUSES OF MARKET VOLATILITY IN OIL TRADING

1. Supply-Demand Imbalances

Demand Fluctuations: Variations in economic growth, seasonal changes, and geopolitical developments can significantly impact global oil consumption. For example, economic booms increase demand for energy, while recessions lead to reduced consumption. Seasonal factors, such as increased travel during summer months or higher heating demand in winter, also affect oil demand. Geopolitical factors, such as international sanctions or changes in trade policies, can lead to sudden shifts in demand patterns.

Supply Disruptions: Geopolitical tensions, natural disasters, and production changes by oil-producing countries can cause significant supply disruptions. Political instability in key oil-producing regions can lead to sudden production halts or reductions. Natural disasters, such as hurricanes in the Gulf of Mexico, can damage infrastructure and halt production. Additionally, strategic decisions by major oil producers, such as production cuts by OPEC, can create supply shortages or surpluses, leading to price volatility.

2. Economic Indicators

GDP Growth: The overall economic health, as indicated by GDP growth, directly affects energy demand and oil prices. Strong economic growth increases industrial activity and transportation needs, driving up oil demand. Conversely, economic slowdowns reduce consumption, leading to lower oil prices.

Inflation Rates: Inflation affects the purchasing power of consumers and the cost of goods and services, including energy. Higher inflation can lead to increased production costs for oil companies and higher energy prices for consumers, while deflation can have the opposite effect. Central bank policies aimed at controlling inflation can also influence oil prices indirectly through their impact on economic growth and currency values.

3. Geopolitical Events

Political Instability: Wars, sanctions, and trade disputes can disrupt global oil supply chains and impact prices. Political instability in oil-rich regions, such as the Middle East, can lead to sudden supply shortages and price spikes. Trade disputes between major economies can affect global supply chains and demand for oil, leading to increased volatility.

Regulatory Changes: Government policies and regulations can significantly influence oil production, distribution, and pricing. Changes in environmental regulations, tax policies, or subsidies for alternative energy sources can affect oil supply and demand dynamics. For example, stricter emissions regulations can increase production costs for oil companies, while subsidies for renewable energy can reduce oil demand.

STRATEGIES FOR MANAGING MARKET VOLATILITY

1 Risk Management

Diversification: One of the fundamental strategies for managing risk in volatile markets is diversification. By spreading investments across different asset classes (such as stocks, bonds, commodities, and real estate) and geographical regions, traders and investors can reduce their exposure to the volatility specific to the oil market. Diversification helps mitigate the impact of adverse price movements in any single market or asset class, leading to a more balanced and resilient portfolio.

Hedging: Hedging involves using financial instruments, such as futures and options contracts, to protect against adverse price movements and manage risk exposure. In the context of oil trading, hedging can help lock in prices for future purchases or sales, thus providing a safeguard against market volatility. For example, an oil producer can sell oil futures to secure current prices for future production, while a consumer can buy oil futures or call options to hedge against rising prices.

2. Technical Analysis

Volatility Indicators: Technical analysis offers several tools to measure and predict price volatility, aiding traders in making informed decisions. Bollinger Bands, for instance, use standard deviation to create bands around a moving average, indicating high and low volatility periods. The Average True Range (ATR) measures the range of price movements over a specific period, providing insights into market volatility. Volatility channels, which use moving averages and volatility measures, help traders identify potential breakouts and market trends.

Chart Patterns: Identifying chart patterns that signify volatility can provide trading opportunities. Patterns such as widening ranges, where price fluctuations become more pronounced, and breakouts, where prices move decisively beyond established support or resistance levels, indicate periods of high volatility. Recognizing these patterns allows traders to capitalize on significant price movements and adjust their strategies accordingly.

3. Fundamental Analysis

Market News: Keeping abreast of market news is essential for understanding the factors driving oil price volatility. Economic reports, such as GDP growth figures, inflation rates, and employment data, provide insights into the broader economic environment affecting oil demand. Geopolitical developments, including conflicts, trade disputes, and regulatory changes, can also have significant impacts on oil prices. Regularly monitoring these sources helps traders anticipate market movements and adjust their positions.

Industry Analysis: Evaluating trends within the oil industry itself is crucial for anticipating market movements. Key factors to consider include changes in oil production levels by major producers, consumption patterns in key markets, and storage capacities. Analyzing supply-demand forecasts and industry reports can provide valuable insights into potential price movements, allowing traders to make more informed decisions.

TOOLS AND RESOURCES FOR MANAGING VOLATILITY

1. Trading Platforms

Features: Selecting the right trading platform is crucial for managing market volatility effectively. Platforms designed for oil trading should offer real-time data feeds, advanced volatility analysis tools, and robust risk management capabilities. These features enable traders to make informed decisions quickly, track market movements accurately, and implement effective risk mitigation strategies.

Examples:

MetaTrader: A popular platform offering a range of technical analysis tools, real-time data, and automated trading capabilities.

Thinkorswim: Known for its comprehensive charting features, customizable alerts, and extensive educational resources.

Interactive Brokers: Provides access to a wide range of markets, advanced trading tools, and risk management features tailored for professional traders.

2. Volatility Measures

Historical Volatility: Analyzing historical price movements helps traders understand past volatility trends and anticipate future market behavior. By examining data over different time frames, traders can identify patterns and periods of high or low volatility, which can inform their trading strategies.

Implied Volatility: Implied volatility, derived from options pricing, reflects the market's expectations of future price fluctuations. Higher implied volatility indicates that traders expect significant price movements, while lower implied volatility suggests more stable market conditions. Monitoring implied volatility helps traders gauge market sentiment and adjust their positions accordingly.

3. Scenario Analysis

Stress Testing: Stress testing involves simulating extreme market conditions to evaluate the resilience of a portfolio. By modeling scenarios such as sudden price drops, geopolitical crises, or significant supply disruptions, traders can assess potential losses and identify weaknesses in their risk management strategies. Stress testing helps prepare for adverse market conditions and ensures that risk mitigation measures are robust.

Sensitivity Analysis: Sensitivity analysis examines how changes in market volatility and economic conditions impact portfolio performance. By modeling different assumptions and scenarios, traders can understand the potential outcomes and adjust their strategies to minimize risk. Sensitivity analysis provides insights into the relationships between various factors and helps traders make more informed decisions under uncertainty.

PSYCHOLOGICAL STRATEGIES FOR DEALING WITH VOLATILITY

Emotional Control: Stick to trading plans and risk management rules during periods of heightened volatility. Practice stress-relief techniques and maintain perspective to avoid impulsive decisions.

Adaptability: Adjust trading strategies and risk exposure based on evolving market conditions and volatility levels.

ADVANTAGES AND CHALLENGES OF VOLATILITY

1. Advantages

Profit Opportunities: Market volatility often leads to rapid and significant price movements, creating numerous trading opportunities. Traders can capitalize on these fluctuations to achieve higher returns. By employing strategies that take advantage of both upward and downward price movements, traders can profit from volatility regardless of market direction.

Market Efficiency: Volatility enhances market efficiency by incorporating new information into prices more rapidly. As market participants react to economic data, geopolitical events, and other factors, prices adjust to reflect this information. This process facilitates price discovery, ensuring that asset prices more accurately reflect their true value based on current market conditions.

2. Challenges

Risk Exposure: While volatility can provide profit opportunities, it also increases the risk of significant losses. Unpredictable price movements and market uncertainty can lead to substantial financial risks for traders. Managing this risk requires robust risk management strategies, such as diversification, hedging, and strict adherence to stop-loss orders.

Emotional Impact: Trading in volatile markets can be psychologically challenging. The rapid and often extreme price swings can induce stress, fear, and overreaction, leading to impulsive decision-making. Traders must maintain emotional control, discipline, and adhere to their trading plans to avoid making decisions based on emotions rather than rational analysis.

Market volatility is inherent in oil trading and presents both opportunities and risks for traders and investors. By understanding the causes of volatility, implementing effective risk management strategies, and utilizing advanced trading tools and resources, traders can navigate and capitalize on market fluctuations.

Techniques such as diversification, hedging, technical and fundamental analysis, and psychological resilience are essential for managing volatility and maintaining profitability in the dynamic oil markets. With continuous learning, adaptation to market conditions, and disciplined execution of trading strategies, traders can mitigate risks and achieve long-term success in oil trading.

CHAPTER 27: PSYCHOLOGICAL ASPECTS OF TRADING: DISCIPLINE AND EMOTIONS

Trading is as much a psychological endeavor as it is a technical and analytical one. The financial markets are influenced by a myriad of factors, many of which are beyond the trader's control. However, one aspect that traders can control is their mindset. This chapter delves into the critical psychological aspects of trading, focusing on the importance of discipline and the management of emotions.

INTRODUCTION TO PSYCHOLOGICAL ASPECTS OF TRADING

Emotional Control: Managing emotions such as fear and greed to make rational trading decisions is paramount. Emotional reactions can cloud judgment, leading to impulsive and often detrimental trading actions. By understanding and controlling these emotions, traders can maintain a level-headed approach to their trades.

Discipline: Sticking to trading plans and risk management strategies amidst market fluctuations is essential for consistent success. Discipline involves following a predefined set of rules and guidelines, regardless of market conditions, to avoid making decisions based on short-term emotional responses.

UNDERSTANDING TRADER PSYCHOLOGY

1. Emotional States

Fear and Greed: These two powerful emotions significantly impact trading behavior. Fear can cause traders to exit positions prematurely or avoid taking necessary risks, while greed can lead to overtrading and taking on excessive risk. Understanding the balance between fear and greed is crucial for maintaining a rational approach to trading.

Overconfidence: Overestimating trading abilities can lead to taking excessive risks and ignoring potential warning signs. Overconfidence often results from a series of successful trades, leading traders to believe they are invincible. Recognizing and mitigating overconfidence can help maintain a realistic perspective on trading performance and risk.

2. Cognitive Biases

Confirmation Bias: This bias involves seeking information that confirms preconceived beliefs and ignoring contradictory evidence. Traders may focus on data that supports their existing positions while disregarding information that suggests they should take a different course of action. Overcoming confirmation bias requires a willingness to objectively evaluate all available information.

Loss Aversion: This cognitive bias reflects a preference for avoiding losses over achieving gains. Traders influenced by loss aversion may hold onto losing positions longer than they should, hoping the market will turn in their favor, or they may avoid taking profitable opportunities due to the fear of potential losses. Recognizing and addressing loss aversion can lead to more balanced and objective trading decisions.

PSYCHOLOGICAL CHALLENGES IN TRADING

Trading in financial markets often exposes traders to various psychological challenges that can significantly impact decision-making and overall performance. Understanding and effectively managing these challenges are crucial for maintaining consistency and success in trading.

1. Fear of Missing Out (FOMO)

Fear of Missing Out refers to the anxiety traders feel about missing potential profit opportunities, which can lead to impulsive trading decisions driven by emotions rather than rational analysis.

Impact: FOMO can compel traders to enter trades hastily, often at less favorable prices or without proper analysis, simply to avoid missing out on what appears to be a profitable opportunity.

Mitigation: To mitigate FOMO, traders should adhere strictly to predefined trading plans and strategies. These plans should include clear entry and exit criteria based on technical or fundamental analysis rather than emotional impulses. By sticking to a disciplined approach, traders can avoid making decisions driven solely by the fear of missing out on potential gains.

2. Loss Aversion

Impact: Loss aversion describes the tendency for traders to prefer avoiding losses over achieving gains, often leading them to hold onto losing positions longer than necessary in the hope that the market will eventually turn in their favor.

Strategy:

Implementing effective risk management practices is essential to mitigate the impact of loss aversion:

Stop-Loss Orders: These are predefined exit points set at levels where the trader is willing to accept a loss. By using stop-loss orders, traders can automate their risk management and prevent emotional decision-making during adverse market conditions.

Adherence to Risk Management Rules: Establishing and adhering to risk management rules, such as limiting the size of each trade relative to the overall portfolio (position sizing), ensures that potential losses are controlled and do not exceed predetermined thresholds.

MAINTAINING DISCIPLINE IN TRADING

Discipline is the cornerstone of successful trading, enabling traders to navigate the uncertainties and challenges of financial markets with a consistent and rational approach.

1. Trading Plan

A trading plan is a detailed strategy that outlines specific criteria for entering and exiting trades, risk tolerance levels, and guidelines for position sizing.

Execution: Successful traders adhere strictly to their trading plans, executing trades based on predefined rules rather than emotions or external influences. This discipline helps maintain consistency in decision-making and reduces the likelihood of making impulsive or irrational trades.

2. Risk Management

Effective risk management is integral to maintaining discipline and protecting capital in trading activities.

Stop-Loss Orders: By setting automated exit points through stop-loss orders, traders ensure that losses are limited to acceptable levels. This prevents emotional decision-making during market fluctuations and preserves capital for future trading opportunities.

Position Sizing: Allocating capital to each trade based on risk tolerance and maintaining consistent risk-reward ratios helps balance potential losses with expected gains. This approach ensures that no single trade can significantly impact the overall portfolio, enhancing long-term sustainability.

TOOLS AND TECHNIQUES FOR EMOTIONAL CONTROL

Emotions play a significant role in trading, influencing decisions and often leading to suboptimal outcomes. Traders who master emotional control can enhance their overall performance and maintain consistency in their trading strategies.

1. Meditation and Mindfulness

Meditation and mindfulness techniques involve practices such as focused breathing, guided meditation, and mindfulness exercises aimed at improving awareness of thoughts and emotions.

Benefits: Traders who incorporate meditation and mindfulness into their routines develop greater emotional resilience and focus. These practices help in reducing stress levels, enhancing concentration during trading sessions, and maintaining emotional balance amidst market fluctuations. By cultivating mindfulness, traders can observe their emotions without reacting impulsively, thereby making more rational trading decisions based on analysis rather than emotions.

2. Journaling

Journaling in trading involves recording detailed insights about each trade, including the rationale behind trading decisions, emotional states during trading, and observations about market conditions.

Reflection: Regularly reviewing and analyzing journal entries allows traders to identify patterns in their behavior and trading outcomes. By reflecting on past trades, traders can pinpoint emotional triggers that led to certain decisions and assess the effectiveness of their trading strategies. Journaling also helps in learning from mistakes and successes, refining trading techniques, and improving overall performance over time.

OVERCOMING PSYCHOLOGICAL BIASES

Psychological biases can significantly impact trading decisions, often leading traders astray from rationality and objective analysis. Overcoming these biases requires awareness, deliberate effort, and the implementation of strategies to mitigate their effects.

AWARENESS:

Identify Biases:

Understanding the various cognitive biases that affect trading decisions is the first step towards overcoming them. Some common biases include:

Anchoring Bias: This bias occurs when traders fixate on a specific reference point, such as the price at which they bought a stock, and base their decisions on this anchor rather than current market conditions.

Herd Mentality: Many traders tend to follow the actions of a larger group or market sentiment rather than making independent decisions based on their own analysis.

Confirmation Bias: This bias leads traders to seek out information that confirms their pre-existing beliefs or trading strategies while disregarding contradictory evidence.

By being aware of these biases, traders can recognize when they are influencing their decision-making process.

Counteract Biases:

Challenge Assumptions: Actively questioning assumptions and initial beliefs is essential. Traders should avoid relying solely on their gut feelings or initial impressions when making trading decisions. Instead, they should seek to validate their assumptions with objective data and analysis.

Seek Diverse Perspectives: Encouraging diverse viewpoints can help counteract biases like confirmation bias. Engaging with different sources of information, considering alternative analyses, and consulting with peers or mentors who may have differing viewpoints can provide a more balanced perspective.

Make Decisions Based on Objective Analysis: Emphasizing data-driven decision-making over emotional impulses is critical. Traders should prioritize objective analysis, technical indicators, and fundamental research when evaluating trade opportunities. This approach helps mitigate biases and ensures decisions are based on factual information rather than emotions.

PSYCHOLOGICAL RESILIENCE AND ADAPTABILITY

Developing psychological resilience and adaptability is essential for traders to navigate the challenges of the financial markets effectively. Here's how traders can cultivate resilience and adaptability in their trading practices:

1. RESILIENCE

Manage Losses: Losses are an inevitable part of trading, and developing resilience involves accepting losses as a natural occurrence rather than a failure. Traders should approach losses with a constructive mindset, focusing on the lessons learned and maintaining confidence in their overall trading strategy. Implementing risk management techniques such as stop-loss orders helps limit losses and reinforces disciplined trading practices.

Focus on Long-Term Profitability: Resilient traders prioritize long-term profitability over short-term setbacks. They understand that individual trades contribute to their overall trading performance and profitability trajectory. By focusing on maintaining consistent profitability over time, traders can mitigate the emotional impact of individual losses and setbacks.

2. ADAPTABILITY

Adjust Trading Strategies:

Adaptability in trading involves the ability to adjust strategies based on changing market conditions and lessons learned from past experiences. Traders should continuously evaluate their trading strategies, identifying strengths and weaknesses, and making necessary adjustments. This adaptability can involve:

Market Analysis: Regularly assessing market trends, economic indicators, and geopolitical events to refine trading strategies accordingly.

Technical Adjustments: Modifying technical analysis tools, such as adjusting moving averages or revising entry and exit points based on current market volatility and price action.

Risk Management Enhancements: Updating risk management practices, such as revising position sizing based on current market conditions or refining stop-loss levels to align with recent market movements.

Learning from Past Experiences: Successful traders leverage past experiences, both successes, and failures, to inform future decision-making. They maintain detailed trading journals to record trade rationale, emotions, and outcomes. By reviewing past trades, traders can identify patterns, refine strategies, and avoid repeating previous mistakes.

SEEKING SUPPORT AND CONTINUOUS IMPROVEMENT

Engaging with trading communities, forums, and seeking mentorship can significantly benefit traders by providing valuable insights, knowledge exchange, and constructive feedback to enhance trading skills and emotional resilience.

COMMUNITY AND MENTORSHIP:

Engage in Trading Communities:

Participating actively in trading communities, whether online forums, social media groups, or local meetups, offers traders opportunities to connect with peers facing similar challenges and opportunities in the financial markets. By engaging in discussions, sharing experiences, and exchanging ideas, traders can gain diverse perspectives on trading strategies, market trends, and risk management techniques.

Seek Mentorship:

Mentorship plays a crucial role in the development of traders, especially those new to the market or seeking to refine their skills. A mentor, typically an experienced trader or industry professional, provides personalized guidance, practical advice, and insights based on their own trading journey. Mentorship relationships often involve:

Knowledge Transfer: Mentors share their expertise, strategies, and lessons learned from their trading experiences.

Skill Development: Mentors offer constructive feedback on trades, helping mentees refine their trading techniques and decision-making processes.

Emotional Support: Mentors provide encouragement and perspective during challenging market conditions, helping mentees maintain focus and resilience.

Feedback for Improvement:

Receiving constructive feedback is essential for traders looking to improve their trading performance and emotional resilience. In trading communities and mentorship relationships, feedback can come from peers, mentors, or through structured trading reviews:

Trade Reviews: Regularly reviewing past trades, discussing trade rationale, outcomes, and areas for improvement helps traders identify strengths and weaknesses in their strategies.

Emotional Resilience: Feedback can also address emotional responses to trading decisions, helping traders develop coping mechanisms and maintain discipline during periods of market volatility or uncertainty.

Benefits of Community and Mentorship:

Learning Opportunities: Access to diverse trading strategies, market insights, and industry trends shared within communities and mentorship relationships accelerates learning and skill development.

Network Building: Building connections with other traders and industry professionals can open doors to new opportunities, collaborations, and access to resources.

Support System: Engaging with a supportive community and having a mentor provides a safety net during challenging times, reducing feelings of isolation and enhancing emotional resilience.

Psychological factors play a critical role in successful trading, influencing decision-making, risk management, and overall trading performance. By understanding and managing emotions, maintaining discipline, and mitigating cognitive biases, traders can enhance their ability to navigate the complexities of financial markets, including oil trading.

PART 10: FUTURE TRENDS IN OIL TRADING

CHAPTER 28: IMPACT OF RENEWABLE ENERGY ON OIL MARKETS

The global energy landscape is undergoing a significant transformation, driven by the growing adoption of renewable energy sources. As countries strive to meet climate goals and reduce dependence on fossil fuels, the impact of renewable energy on oil markets becomes increasingly pronounced. This chapter delves into the dynamics between renewable energy developments and the traditional oil market, exploring how advancements in solar, wind, and other clean energy technologies influence oil demand, pricing, and industry strategies.

ENERGY TRANSITION

The global energy landscape is witnessing a significant shift as renewable energy sources gain prominence. This transition is driven by the urgent need to address climate change, reduce greenhouse gas emissions, and enhance energy security. The move towards renewables is reshaping the dynamics of the oil markets, influencing demand patterns, pricing mechanisms, and investment strategies. Understanding this shift is crucial for stakeholders in the energy sector to navigate the evolving market landscape.

Market Dynamics

The adoption of renewable energy sources is accelerating due to several key factors:

Technological Advancements: Innovations in renewable energy technologies, such as more efficient solar panels and wind turbines, are reducing costs and increasing the competitiveness of renewables compared to traditional fossil fuels.

Policy Initiatives: Governments worldwide are implementing policies and regulations to promote renewable energy adoption. These include subsidies, tax incentives, and renewable energy mandates, which are designed to reduce reliance on oil and other fossil fuels.

Consumer Preferences: Increasing awareness of environmental issues and the desire for cleaner energy options are driving consumers and businesses to opt for renewable energy solutions over traditional oil-based products.

GROWTH OF RENEWABLE ENERGY SOURCES

1. RENEWABLE ENERGY TECHNOLOGIES

Solar and Wind Power

Solar and wind power have seen substantial growth in recent years, with significant investments in these sectors:

Expansion of Solar Photovoltaic (PV) Capacity: The cost of solar PV technology has decreased dramatically, making it a viable option for large-scale electricity generation and residential use. Countries around the world are increasing their solar capacity to reduce dependence on oil-based power generation.

Wind Energy Growth: Wind power has also expanded rapidly, driven by technological improvements and government incentives. Offshore wind projects are becoming more common, adding to the renewable energy mix and further reducing oil demand for power generation.

Electric Vehicles (EVs)

The transportation sector is undergoing a transformation with the increasing adoption of electric vehicles:

Adoption Trends: EV sales are growing globally, supported by advancements in battery technology, increased vehicle range, and the development of charging infrastructure.

Government Incentives: Many governments are offering incentives such as tax breaks, rebates, and subsidies to encourage the purchase of EVs, aiming to reduce oil consumption and lower emissions.

Market Penetration: The penetration of EVs into the automotive market is increasing, with projections indicating that EVs will comprise a significant portion of the global vehicle fleet in the coming decades. This shift is expected to have a profound impact on oil demand, particularly for gasoline and diesel.

IMPACT ON OIL DEMAND

1. TRANSPORTATION SECTOR

Fuel Substitution

The substitution of traditional fossil fuels with renewable alternatives in the transportation sector is a key factor in reducing oil demand:

Biofuels and Hydrogen: Biofuels and hydrogen are emerging as alternative fuels that can replace gasoline and diesel in internal combustion engines and fuel cell vehicles, respectively. Their adoption is being driven by the need to reduce carbon emissions and enhance energy security.

Hybrid Vehicles: Hybrid vehicles, which combine internal combustion engines with electric propulsion, are also contributing to the reduction in oil demand. They offer improved fuel efficiency and lower emissions, acting as a bridge technology towards full electrification.

Electric Vehicles

The growth of electric vehicles is having a significant impact on gasoline and diesel consumption patterns:

Decline in Gasoline Demand: As more consumers switch to EVs, the demand for gasoline is expected to decline. This shift is particularly pronounced in regions with strong EV adoption rates and supportive government policies.

Reduced Diesel Consumption: The adoption of electric trucks and buses is also reducing diesel consumption in the commercial transportation sector. This trend is expected to continue as battery technology improves and charging infrastructure expands.

TECHNOLOGICAL ADVANCEMENTS

1. ENERGY EFFICIENCY

Technological Innovations

Technological advancements are crucial in enhancing energy efficiency and integrating renewable energy into existing systems:

Energy Storage: Innovations in battery storage technology allow for better storage and distribution of renewable energy, addressing the intermittency issues of solar and wind power. Improved energy storage solutions enable a more reliable and stable energy supply, reducing dependency on oil-based backup power.

Smart Grid Technologies: Smart grids incorporate digital communication technology to monitor and manage energy flow, increasing the efficiency and reliability of the electricity distribution network. This optimization reduces energy waste and facilitates the integration of renewable energy sources.

Renewable Energy Integration: Technological developments in grid integration enable a seamless blend of renewable energy with traditional power sources. Improved grid management systems, inverters, and converters help accommodate the variable output of renewables, ensuring a steady energy supply and reducing the need for oil-based power generation.

Impact on Energy Markets

The integration of renewable energy into grid systems significantly influences energy pricing dynamics:

Energy Market Transformation: As renewable energy becomes more cost-effective and widespread, it exerts downward pressure on energy prices. The decreased demand for oil in power generation affects the overall market value of fossil fuels.

Price Volatility: The increasing share of renewables introduces variability in energy supply, which can lead to price fluctuations. However, advancements in storage and grid technologies are mitigating these effects, creating a more balanced and predictable energy market.

INVESTOR PREFERENCES AND MARKET SENTIMENT

1. ESG INVESTING

Investor Trends

Environmental, social, and governance (ESG) criteria are reshaping investment strategies:

Shift Towards ESG Criteria: Investors are increasingly considering ESG factors in their decision-making processes. This trend favors investments in renewable energy projects that align with sustainability goals and demonstrate strong governance practices.

Divestment from Fossil Fuels: Many institutional investors are divesting from oil and other fossil fuels, reallocating capital towards cleaner energy alternatives. This shift is driven by both ethical considerations and the recognition of long-term financial risks associated with fossil fuel investments.

Financial Markets

Investor sentiment and capital flows have profound effects on the oil sector:

Impact on Investments: As more capital flows into renewable energy projects, the oil sector experiences a relative decrease in investment. This shift impacts the ability of oil companies to finance new exploration and production activities.

Valuation Changes: The market valuation of oil companies is influenced by investor sentiment. Companies perceived as lagging in sustainability efforts may face reduced market capitalization and higher borrowing costs, while those investing in renewable technologies may see improved valuations and investor confidence.

GEOPOLITICAL CONSIDERATIONS

1. ENERGY INDEPENDENCE

Energy Security

Energy security is a crucial aspect of national policy, and the diversification of energy sources significantly enhances it:

Diversification of Energy Sources: By adopting renewable energy sources, countries can reduce their dependence on oil imports, enhancing their energy security. This diversification minimizes the risks associated with supply disruptions caused by geopolitical tensions, trade disputes, or natural disasters.

Reduction of Reliance on Oil Imports: Reducing oil imports can alter a country's geopolitical strategies and alliances. Nations less dependent on oil imports are better positioned to pursue independent foreign policies without being influenced by oil-exporting countries. This shift can lead to realignments in international relations and changes in global power dynamics.

Global Supply Chains

The adoption of renewable energy affects global supply chains and necessitates new infrastructure investments:

Changes in Energy Supply Chains: As the world transitions to renewable energy, the traditional supply chains for oil are being reconfigured. The transportation, storage, and distribution networks for oil are evolving to accommodate new energy sources like solar, wind, and bioenergy.

Infrastructure Investments: Significant investments in renewable energy infrastructure are required to support this transition. This includes building new power plants, upgrading grid systems, and developing storage solutions. These investments can create new economic opportunities and reshape global energy markets.

FUTURE TRENDS AND FORECAST

1. ENERGY OUTLOOK

Long-term Projections

Forecasts for the energy sector indicate significant changes in the coming decades:

Renewable Energy Growth: Renewable energy sources, particularly solar and wind, are expected to continue their rapid growth. Advancements in technology, decreasing costs, and supportive government policies will drive this expansion, leading to a larger share of renewables in the global energy mix.

Oil Demand Trends: While oil demand may decline in the long term due to the adoption of electric vehicles and energy efficiency measures, it will still play a role in the global energy landscape. Demand will likely shift from transportation fuels to petrochemicals and other industrial uses.

Market Dynamics: Technological advancements, such as improved battery storage and grid integration, will influence energy markets. Additionally, policy shifts towards decarbonization and climate change mitigation will shape future energy demand and supply dynamics.

Scenario Analysis

Different scenarios can be envisaged for the future of oil markets, depending on various factors:

High Transition Scenario: In a scenario where the world aggressively pursues renewable energy adoption and stringent climate policies, oil demand could see a steep decline. This would lead to significant investments in clean energy technologies and a rapid shift away from fossil fuels.

Moderate Transition Scenario: A more gradual transition scenario would see continued reliance on oil in the short to medium term, with a steady increase in renewable energy capacity. Oil companies would balance their portfolios with investments in both fossil fuels and renewables.

Low Transition Scenario: In a scenario with slower renewable energy adoption and less stringent climate policies, oil demand might remain relatively stable. This could result in prolonged dependence on oil, with incremental improvements in energy efficiency and carbon capture technologies.

The transition towards renewable energy sources represents a transformative shift in global energy markets, impacting the demand, pricing, and strategic outlook for oil.

CHAPTER 29: TECHNOLOGICAL ADVANCEMENTS IN TRADING

The landscape of trading has undergone significant transformations in recent years, driven by rapid technological advancements. From high-frequency trading algorithms to sophisticated risk management tools, technology has reshaped the way financial markets operate and how traders interact with them.

This chapter delves into the pivotal role of technology in modern trading, exploring the tools, platforms, and innovations that have revolutionized the industry.

EVOLUTION OF TRADING TECHNOLOGIES

The trading landscape has been dramatically transformed by a series of technological innovations. This section will explore how these advancements have revolutionized trading practices and strategies. From the advent of electronic trading platforms to the rise of artificial intelligence and machine learning, we will trace the technological evolution that has redefined market operations.

Impact: Technological advancements in trading have brought numerous benefits, including increased trading efficiency, improved risk management, and enhanced market liquidity. However, these innovations also pose challenges, such as the potential for market manipulation and the need for robust cybersecurity measures. We will analyze the positive impacts as well as the potential pitfalls and future implications of these technological shifts in trading.

ALGORITHMIC TRADING AND QUANTITATIVE STRATEGIES

Algorithmic Trading

Automation: Algorithmic trading involves using computer programs and algorithms to automate trading activities. These systems execute trades based on predefined criteria, such as timing, price, and volume. Automation minimizes human error, increases trading speed, and allows for the execution of complex strategies that are impossible to achieve manually.

Quantitative Models: The backbone of algorithmic trading is the development of sophisticated quantitative models. These models employ mathematical and statistical techniques to analyze market data, identify trading signals, and make informed trading decisions. Quantitative strategies can include statistical arbitrage, market making, and trend following, each tailored to exploit specific market conditions.

HIGH-FREQUENCY TRADING (HFT) AND MARKET LIQUIDITY

HFT Strategies Speed and Efficiency:

High-Frequency Trading (HFT) is characterized by the execution of a large number of trades at extremely high speeds, often within microseconds. HFT strategies capitalize on small price differentials, leveraging speed and efficiency to generate profits from tiny market movements. This requires state-of-the-art technology and access to ultra-fast trading platforms.

Liquidity Provision: HFT plays a critical role in enhancing market liquidity. By continually buying and selling securities, HFT firms contribute to tighter bid-ask spreads and more efficient price discovery. However, the high-speed nature of HFT also raises concerns about market stability and the potential for flash crashes, making the regulation of HFT a topic of ongoing debate.

ARTIFICIAL INTELLIGENCE (AI) AND MACHINE LEARNING

AI Applications Predictive Analytics:

AI algorithms are increasingly used for market forecasting and trend identification. Predictive analytics involves analyzing historical market data and using machine learning models to predict future price movements. These AI-driven insights enable traders to anticipate market trends and make more informed trading decisions.

Pattern Recognition: Machine learning techniques are adept at analyzing large datasets to recognize complex patterns that may not be evident through traditional analysis. By identifying these patterns, AI can uncover hidden trading opportunities, optimize entry and exit points, and enhance overall trading strategy performance. This capability is particularly valuable in volatile markets like oil trading, where rapid and informed decision-making is crucial.

BLOCKCHAIN TECHNOLOGY AND DISTRIBUTED LEDGER SYSTEMS

Transparency and Security

Decentralization: Blockchain technology's decentralized nature ensures that no single entity has control over the entire system. This decentralization enhances security by reducing the risk of single points of failure and making it difficult for malicious actors to alter transaction records. Each transaction is recorded in a block, which is then linked to the previous block, creating an immutable chain of transactions that is transparent and secure.

Smart Contracts: Smart contracts are self-executing contracts with the terms of the agreement directly written into code. They automatically execute and enforce the terms of a contract when predefined conditions are met. In trading, smart contracts can streamline processes such as trade settlements, clearing, and compliance, reducing the need for intermediaries and minimizing the risk of human error or fraud. This automation leads to faster, more efficient, and more reliable transactions.

BIG DATA ANALYTICS AND REAL-TIME MARKET INSIGHTS

Data Integration

Data Sources: Big data analytics in trading involves integrating various data streams, including traditional market data (such as price, volume, and order book data), news feeds, economic indicators, and social media sentiment. Advanced data integration techniques allow traders to consolidate these diverse data sources into a unified analytical framework, providing a comprehensive view of market dynamics.

Decision Support: Utilizing big data analytics enables traders to gain real-time market insights that support informed decision-making. Analytical tools can process vast amounts of data quickly, identifying trends, correlations, and anomalies that may not be apparent through manual analysis. Predictive analytics and machine learning models can forecast market movements, helping traders develop strategies based on data-driven insights and improving the accuracy and speed of their decision-making processes.

CLOUD COMPUTING AND INFRASTRUCTURE

Scalability and Flexibility

Cloud Services: The deployment of trading platforms and infrastructure on cloud-based solutions offers significant advantages in terms of scalability and cost-efficiency. Cloud services allow trading firms to scale their operations up or down based on demand without the need for significant upfront investment in physical infrastructure. This flexibility is particularly beneficial in high-frequency trading environments where computational power and storage needs can vary greatly.

Remote Access: Cloud computing enhances operational agility by enabling remote access to trading systems and data analytics tools from any location with internet connectivity. This accessibility allows traders to monitor markets, execute trades, and analyze data in real-time, regardless of their physical location. Cloud-based infrastructure also facilitates collaboration among team members across different geographical locations, improving the efficiency and effectiveness of trading operations.

Technological advancements continue to redefine trading practices, offering new opportunities for efficiency, innovation, and risk management in oil and financial markets.

PART 11: RESOURCES AND FURTHER READING

CHAPTER 30: RECOMMENDED RESOURCES

In the constantly evolving landscape of trading, staying informed and continually expanding your knowledge is essential for success. The trading industry is rich with literature, offering a wealth of insights from seasoned professionals, academic experts, and market theorists.

This chapter curates a list of recommended resources – books, online courses and articles that provide valuable perspectives on various aspects of trading, including algorithmic trading, market psychology, risk management, and the impact of emerging technologies.

BOOKS ON OIL TRADING

Oil 101 by Morgan Downey: An introductory guide covering the fundamentals of the oil industry, trading strategies, and market dynamics.

Trading Oil Manual by Owain Johnson: Insights into practical aspects of oil trading, risk management, and trading strategies in global markets.

ONLINE COURSES AND TUTORIALS

Investopedia Academy - Energy Trading Course: Comprehensive introduction to energy markets, oil trading strategies, and risk management techniques.

Coursera - Introduction to Oil and Gas: Understanding global energy markets, supply chain dynamics, and economic factors influencing oil prices.

FINANCIAL MARKET ANALYSIS

Technical Analysis of the Financial Markets by John J. Murphy: Classic reference on technical analysis techniques, chart patterns, and trading strategies.

A Random Walk Down Wall Street by Burton G. Malkiel: Overview of investment strategies, market efficiency, and portfolio management principles.

ENERGY ECONOMICS AND POLICY

Energy Trading and Investing by Davis Edwards: Exploration of energy markets, trading strategies, and risk management in global energy commodities.

The Prize: The Epic Quest for Oil, Money, and Power by Daniel Yergin: Historical perspective on the oil industry, geopolitical influences, and economic impact.

QUANTITATIVE FINANCE AND ALGORITHMIC TRADING

Algorithmic Trading: Winning Strategies and Their Rationale by Ernie Chan: Application of quantitative techniques, algorithmic trading strategies, and risk management.

Advances in Financial Machine Learning by Marcos López de Prado: Cutting-edge insights into machine learning applications, big data analytics, and financial market forecasting.

ACADEMIC JOURNALS AND RESEARCH ARTICLES

Journal of Energy Markets: Peer-reviewed research on energy market dynamics, pricing models, and policy implications.

Journal of Finance: Leading academic research on financial markets, investment strategies, and empirical studies on market efficiency.

INDUSTRY REPORTS AND MARKET UPDATES

Oil Price Information Service (OPIS): Market analysis, price forecasts, and industry trends in global oil markets.

Bloomberg Energy: Insights into energy market trends, commodity prices, and geopolitical developments impacting oil trading.

ONLINE RESOURCES AND NEWS PLATFORMS

Financial Times: Coverage of global financial markets, economic trends, and industry-specific news on oil and commodities.

Reuters Energy News: Real-time updates, market analysis, and expert commentary on energy markets and oil trading strategies.

Recommended resources serve as valuable resources for deepening knowledge, refining trading strategies, and staying informed about evolving trends in oil trading and financial markets.

Exploring authoritative texts, academic journals, industry reports, and online resources, helps enhance your understanding of market dynamics, leverage advanced trading techniques, and navigate complexities in global energy markets effectively.

Continuous learning, exploration of diverse perspectives, and engagement with industry experts contribute to professional development and strategic decision-making in the dynamic landscape of oil trading and financial markets.

CHAPTER 31: INDUSTRY REPORTS AND MARKET DATA SOURCES

Accurate and timely information is the cornerstone of effective trading. In Chapter 31, we explore the essential industry reports and market data sources that traders rely on to make informed decisions. Access to high-quality data and comprehensive analysis allows traders to understand market trends, evaluate economic indicators, and anticipate price movements.

This chapter provides a curated list of reputable sources for industry reports and market data, covering various aspects of the trading world, including commodities, equities, forex, and derivatives. From government publications and industry associations to private financial institutions and independent research firms, these sources offer invaluable insights into market dynamics, economic forecasts, and sector-specific developments.

OIL MARKET REPORTS

IEA Oil Market Report: Monthly updates on global oil supply, demand forecasts, and market balances influencing oil prices.

OPEC Monthly Oil Market Report: Insights into OPEC production levels, market trends, and geopolitical factors impacting oil markets.

COMMODITY PRICE PLATFORMS

Bloomberg Energy Prices: Real-time updates on crude oil, refined products, and natural gas prices, along with market commentary and analysis.

Platts Oil Price Assessments: Price assessments, market intelligence, and news covering oil and energy markets globally.

FINANCIAL MARKET DATA PROVIDERS

Reuters Market Data: Comprehensive coverage of financial markets, commodities, and economic indicators influencing trading decisions.

MarketWatch: News, analysis, and stock market data for tracking energy stocks, commodities, and market trends.

GOVERNMENT AND REGULATORY REPORTS

U.S. Energy Information Administration (EIA): Reports on energy production, consumption, and forecasts impacting global energy markets.

European Commission - Directorate-General for Energy: Market analysis, energy policies, and regulatory updates affecting European energy markets.

INDUSTRY ASSOCIATIONS AND RESEARCH ORGANIZATIONS

American Petroleum Institute (API): Industry statistics, standards, and economic analysis related to the oil and natural gas sectors in the United States.

International Energy Agency (IEA): Energy market analysis, forecasts, and policy recommendations for member countries and global energy markets.

TRADE PUBLICATIONS AND MARKET ANALYSIS

Oil & Gas Journal: News, data, and analysis on upstream, midstream, and downstream sectors of the oil and gas industry.

Energy Intelligence Group: Reports, newsletters, and market analysis focusing on global energy markets, geopolitical developments, and industry trends.

ONLINE DATABASES AND RESEARCH PLATFORMS

Thomson Reuters Eikon: Financial market data, analytics, and news for research, trading, and risk management in oil and commodity markets.

S&P Global Platts Analytics: Market intelligence, forecasts, and insights on energy commodities, pricing trends, and supply chain dynamics.

Industry reports and reliable market data sources play a crucial role in shaping informed decision-making, risk management strategies, and trading operations in oil and financial markets. By accessing authoritative reports, price assessments, and economic analyses from reputable sources, traders can stay updated on market trends, regulatory developments, and geopolitical factors influencing energy prices.

Continuous monitoring of industry publications, government reports, and financial market data platforms enhances traders' ability to identify opportunities, mitigate risks, and optimize performance

PART 12: CONCLUSION AND NEXT STEPS

CHAPTER 32: RECAP OF KEY CONCEPTS

This chapter serves as a comprehensive summary of the critical concepts covered throughout the book, reinforcing your understanding and ensuring you have a solid foundation for successful oil trading. Here's a quick recap of each part:

PART 1: INTRODUCTION TO OIL TRADING

- **Overview of the Oil Market:** Understand the structure and types of crude oil, like Brent and WTI.

- **Importance of Oil:** Recognize oil's role in the global economy and its price impacts.

- **Different Types of Oil:** Learn the unique characteristics and pricing of Brent and WTI.

PART 2: FUNDAMENTALS OF OIL TRADING

- **Supply and Demand Dynamics:** Grasp the factors driving oil prices.

- **Key Players:** Identify OPEC, non-OPEC producers, and speculators.

- **Impact of Geopolitical Events:** Stay informed about global events affecting oil prices.

PART 3: OIL MARKET INSTRUMENTS

- **Oil CFDs:** Speculate on price movements without owning oil.

- **Oil Futures:** Use contracts to buy/sell oil at a predetermined price/date.

- **Oil Options:** Gain the right, but not the obligation, to buy/sell oil at a specific price.

PART 4: MARKET ANALYSIS TECHNIQUES

- **Fundamental Analysis:** Evaluate supply-demand factors and geopolitical events.

- **Technical Analysis:** Use charts and indicators to identify trading opportunities.

- **Sentiment Analysis:** Gauge market psychology to anticipate price changes.

PART 5: TRADING PLATFORMS AND TOOLS

- **Choosing the Right Platform:** Select a reliable platform with robust features.

- **Specialized Trading Tools:** Enhance trading efficiency with various tools.

- **Trading Software and Apps:** Use mobile apps for flexible trading.

PART 6: DEVELOPING A TRADING STRATEGY

- **Setting Trading Goals:** Establish clear and realistic goals.

- **Risk Management:** Protect capital with stop-loss orders and position sizing.

- **Creating a Trading Plan:** Outline entry/exit criteria, risk tolerance, and rules.

PART 7: EXECUTING TRADES

- **Placing Orders:** Understand market, limit, and stop-loss orders.

- **Spreads and Leverage:** Know the impact on trading costs and returns.
- **Managing Open Positions:** Monitor and adjust positions for optimal outcomes.

PART 8: ADVANCED TRADING STRATEGIES

- **Spread Trading:** Profit from price differentials in different contracts.
- **Hedging:** Protect against adverse price movements.
- **Swing and Day Trading:** Capitalize on short-term price movements.

PART 9: RISK MANAGEMENT AND PSYCHOLOGY

- **Identifying Risks:** Recognize and mitigate potential risks.
- **Dealing with Volatility:** Manage and make informed decisions amid volatility.
- **Psychological Aspects:** Control emotions and maintain discipline.

PART 10: FUTURE TRENDS IN OIL TRADING

- **Renewable Energy Impact:** Understand how the energy transition affects oil markets.
- **Technological Advancements:** Explore innovations like algorithmic trading and AI.

PART 11: RESOURCES AND FURTHER READING

- **Recommended Resources:** Further reading to deepen your knowledge.
- **Industry Reports:** Essential reports and data sources for informed trading.

PART 12: CONCLUSION AND NEXT STEPS

- **Recap of Key Concepts:** Reinforce essential knowledge.
- **Final Tips:** Practical advice for navigating oil markets.
- **Continuous Learning:** Emphasize the importance of staying updated.

This chapter consolidates your understanding of oil trading, ensuring you're equipped with the knowledge and tools needed for successful trading endeavors.

CHAPTER 33: FINAL TIPS FOR ASPIRING OIL TRADERS

As we approach the culmination of this comprehensive guide on oil trading, it's time to distill the essential wisdom and practical advice that will support your journey from novice to proficient trader. In this chapter, we'll provide you with a collection of final tips designed to help you navigate the complexities of the oil market with confidence and strategic acumen.

Whether you're just beginning to explore the fascinating world of oil trading or looking to refine your existing strategies, these tips will serve as a valuable reference. We'll cover critical aspects such as maintaining discipline, leveraging the right resources, adapting to market changes, and continuously learning and improving.

BUILD A STRONG FOUNDATION

Continuous Learning: Staying updated with industry trends, market dynamics, and trading strategies is crucial for success in oil trading. Regularly engage with educational resources such as books, online courses, webinars, and professional certifications. Joining industry forums and networking with experienced traders can also provide valuable insights and perspectives.

Master the Basics: A thorough understanding of fundamental concepts is essential. Make sure you have a solid grasp of oil markets, including the key players, supply and demand dynamics, and geopolitical factors. Familiarize yourself with different trading instruments like CFDs, futures, and options, and master various market analysis techniques, both fundamental and technical.

DEVELOP A TRADING STRATEGY

Strategy Development

Define Objectives: Clearly defined objectives are the cornerstone of any successful trading strategy. Set specific trading goals, determine your risk tolerance levels, and establish financial targets. These objectives will serve as a roadmap for your trading decisions, helping you stay focused and disciplined.

Choose Your Approach: Based on your strengths and preferences, decide whether you will focus on fundamental analysis, technical analysis, or a combination of both. Fundamental analysis involves evaluating economic indicators, industry trends, and geopolitical events, while technical analysis relies on charts and indicators to identify trading opportunities. Combining both approaches can provide a more comprehensive view of the market and enhance your decision-making process.

UNDERSTAND RISK MANAGEMENT

Risk Assessment

Position Sizing: Proper position sizing is a critical component of risk management. Calculate the optimal trade size based on your risk tolerance and the total capital you have allocated for trading. Avoid over-leveraging, as this can lead to significant losses. By sizing your positions correctly, you can ensure that no single trade will have a disproportionate impact on your overall portfolio.

Use Stop-Loss Orders: Implementing stop-loss orders is a fundamental risk management practice. These orders automatically sell your position when the price reaches a predetermined level, limiting potential losses. This helps protect your capital, especially in volatile market conditions, and prevents emotional decision-making that can lead to larger-than-expected losses.

EMBRACE TECHNOLOGY AND TOOLS

Utilize Trading Platforms

Choose Wisely: Select trading platforms that are reliable, user-friendly, and equipped with essential features such as real-time data, advanced charting capabilities, and efficient order execution. The right platform can greatly enhance your trading experience by providing the tools and information needed to make informed decisions quickly and accurately.

Explore Automation: Consider incorporating algorithmic trading strategies and AI-driven analytics into your trading routine. Automated trading can help execute trades based on predefined criteria, removing emotional bias and improving consistency. Additionally, leveraging technical indicators and AI algorithms can provide deeper insights into market trends and help identify profitable trading opportunities.

MONITOR MARKET TRENDS AND NEWS

Stay Informed

Follow Market News: Staying informed about current events is crucial for successful trading. Keep track of geopolitical developments, economic data releases, and industry-specific news that can impact oil prices and market sentiment. Subscribing to financial news services and participating in industry forums can help you stay updated with the latest information.

Use Market Analysis: Regularly conduct market analysis using both fundamental and technical tools. Fundamental analysis involves assessing economic indicators, company performance, and geopolitical events, while technical analysis focuses on price patterns and statistical indicators. By combining both approaches, you can gain a comprehensive understanding of the market and better anticipate price movements, identifying trading opportunities and potential risks.

CULTIVATE DISCIPLINE AND PATIENCE

Psychological Preparedness

Stick to Your Plan: Adhering to your trading strategy is essential for long-term success. Avoid making impulsive decisions based on emotions, especially during periods of market volatility. By sticking to your predefined plan, you can maintain consistency and reduce the risk of costly mistakes.

Exercise Patience: Recognize that successful trading requires time, practice, and a long-term perspective. Be patient with your progress and understand that consistent results come from disciplined execution and continuous learning. Patience will help you avoid the temptation of chasing quick profits and instead focus on sustainable growth.

NETWORK AND LEARN FROM EXPERTS

Industry Insights

Join Communities: Engage with fellow traders by participating in online forums, social media groups, and industry conferences. These communities provide valuable opportunities to exchange ideas, discuss strategies, and gain insights from other traders' experiences. Networking can also help you stay updated on market trends and new trading techniques.

Seek Mentorship: Learning from seasoned traders or mentors can accelerate your growth as a trader. Seek out mentors who can provide guidance, share their strategies, and offer constructive feedback on your trading approach. A mentor's experience and insights can help you navigate challenges and refine your skills more effectively.

Manage Your Expectations

Realistic Goals

Start Small: Begin with manageable investments and gradually scale your trading activities as you gain experience and confidence. Starting small allows you to learn the ropes without risking significant capital, helping you build a solid foundation before taking on larger positions.

Accept Risks: Understand that trading involves inherent risks, and losses are a natural part of the learning process. Accepting this reality will help you maintain a balanced perspective and avoid becoming discouraged by setbacks. Focus on learning from your losses and continuously improving your trading strategies to become a proficient oil trader.

Aspiring oil traders can navigate the complexities of energy markets and enhance their trading skills by following these final tips. By building a solid foundation of knowledge, developing a clear trading strategy, practicing effective risk management, leveraging technology, and staying informed about market trends, traders can increase their chances of success.

Cultivating discipline, patience, and continuous learning are crucial for adapting to market changes and refining trading techniques over time. Networking with industry professionals and seeking mentorship further accelerates learning and provides valuable insights into effective trading practices. Ultimately, managing expectations and maintaining a realistic outlook on trading outcomes are essential for achieving sustainable growth and profitability in the competitive landscape of oil trading.

CHAPTER 34: ENCOURAGEMENT FOR CONTINUOUS LEARNING

In the fast-paced and ever-evolving world of oil trading, the importance of continuous learning cannot be overstated. As market dynamics, trading technologies, and industry regulations constantly shift, staying ahead of the curve requires a commitment to ongoing education and skill development.

This final chapter aims to inspire and motivate you to embrace a lifelong learning mindset, highlighting the benefits of continuous improvement and offering practical advice on how to keep your knowledge and skills up-to-date. By fostering a culture of learning, you can adapt to changes more effectively, enhance your trading strategies, and ultimately achieve greater success in your trading endeavors.

THE POWER OF KNOWLEDGE

Lifelong Growth

Commit to Learning: Developing a habit of consistent learning is crucial. Prioritize expanding your knowledge base through various sources, including books, online courses, seminars, and industry-specific resources. Continuous education helps in staying relevant and competitive.

Stay Curious: Curiosity drives discovery and innovation. Embrace a curious mindset to delve into new concepts, stay abreast of emerging trends, and explore innovative trading strategies within the oil markets. This proactive approach fosters a deeper understanding and sparks creative solutions..

EVOLVING INDUSTRY DYNAMICS

Adaptability

Stay Updated: Keep pace with technological advancements, regulatory changes, and geopolitical developments shaping global energy markets. The oil trading environment is influenced by numerous external factors, and being well-informed allows traders to make timely and informed decisions. Subscribe to industry newsletters, follow market news, and participate in webinars and conferences to stay updated.

Flexibility: Adapt trading strategies and approaches based on evolving market conditions and emerging opportunities. Flexibility is a key trait for successful traders, allowing them to adjust their tactics in response to market shifts. Regularly review and refine your trading strategies to ensure they remain effective in changing conditions.

PROFESSIONAL DEVELOPMENT

Skill Enhancement

Continuous Improvement: Seek opportunities to enhance trading skills, refine analytical techniques, and adopt best practices in risk management. Continuous improvement is essential for staying competitive in the oil trading industry. Attend advanced training sessions, pursue certifications, and engage in practical exercises to hone your skills.

Networking: Engage with industry peers, attend workshops, and participate in professional forums to exchange ideas and insights. Building a strong professional network provides access to diverse perspectives and valuable knowledge. Join trading communities, attend industry events, and actively participate in discussions to expand your network and learn from others.

EMBRACING INNOVATION

Technological Integration

Leverage Technology: The integration of advanced technologies is transforming trading practices. Embrace tools like algorithmic trading platforms, AI-driven analytics, and big data solutions to gain a competitive edge. These technologies offer enhanced analytical capabilities, real-time insights, and efficient execution of trading strategies.

Innovative Strategies: Stay ahead of the curve by exploring and incorporating innovative trading methodologies. Experiment with new approaches and technologies to optimize your trading performance. Being open to innovation allows you to capitalize on cutting-edge developments and maintain a strategic advantage.

OVERCOMING CHALLENGES

Resilience

Learn from Setbacks: View challenges as opportunities for growth, resilience, and refining your trading approach. Setbacks and losses are inevitable in trading, but they can be valuable learning experiences. Analyzing what went wrong and why can provide insights that help improve future performance. Embrace these moments as critical for personal and professional development.

Persistence: Persevere through market fluctuations, learn from mistakes, and maintain a long-term perspective on achieving trading success. Trading requires a steadfast mindset and the ability to weather both high and low periods. Persistence and a focus on long-term goals will help maintain momentum even when short-term outcomes are unfavorable. Consistent effort and dedication are essential for achieving sustained success.

CULTIVATING MENTORSHIP

Learning from Experts

Seek Guidance: Benefit from mentorship, guidance, and insights from experienced traders who can provide valuable perspectives and advice. Experienced traders have navigated the complexities of the market and can offer invaluable advice on strategies, risk management, and psychological aspects of trading. Seeking mentorship can accelerate learning and provide practical insights that are not readily available through books or courses.

Peer Collaboration: Engage with peers, share experiences, and collaborate on learning initiatives to foster mutual growth and support. Collaborating with fellow traders allows for the exchange of ideas, strategies, and experiences. This mutual support can lead to a deeper understanding of market dynamics and collective problem-solving. Participating in study groups, forums, and networking events can create a supportive community that enhances learning and trading effectiveness.

Continuous learning is not just a pathway to success in oil trading but a lifelong commitment to personal and professional growth. By embracing a mindset of curiosity, adaptability, and innovation, aspiring traders can navigate the complexities of energy markets with confidence and resilience.

Through ongoing education, skill enhancement, and collaboration with industry peers and mentors, traders can stay ahead of the curve, capitalize on emerging opportunities, and achieve sustainable success in the competitive landscape of global energy trading.

ABOUT THE AUTHOR

Usiere Uko

Usiere Uko is a Consultant, ILO Certified Trainer, and Business & Finance Author focused on financial independence and entrepreneurship. A former oil and gas engineer turned entrepreneur, he helps individuals and business owners build sustainable income, make smarter financial decisions, and grow resilient businesses.

He is a certified Business Development Service Provider (BDSP) and an ILO-certified trainer in SIYB and WIDB, and currently serves as Lead Consultant at Sageway Consulting and Training Coordinator at The Citadel Business Academy.

Usiere writes in a friendly and practical style, making complex financial and business ideas simple, clear, and actionable for everyday readers and entrepreneurs. He is based in Lagos, Nigeria.

BOOKS IN THIS SERIES
COMMODITIES TRADING FOR BEGINNERS

Gold Trading 101: The Beginner's Guide To Unlocking The Potential Of Precious Metals

Silver Trading 101: Smart Strategies For Silver Trading Beginners

Oil Trading 101: Understanding The Basics Of Trading The Oil Market, Cfds, Futures And Options

Natural Gas Trading 101: A Beginner's Guide To Profiting From The Energy Market

BOOKS BY THIS AUTHOR

Practical Steps To Financial Freedom And Independence: Money Management Skills For Beginners

Before You Trade Forex: Things You Need To Know If You Desire To Start Trading Forex Profitably

Before You Invest In Cryptocurrency: A Simple Guide To Understanding The Cryptocurrency Market

101 Common Money Mistakes To Avoid: And How To Fix Them. Book 1: Expenses. Money Management, Making Your Budget Work

How To Avoid Living Under Financial Pressure: A Simple Guide To Getting Back Control Of Your Finances

Financial Independence For Employees: Making

Your Job A Stepping Stone To Exiting The Rat Race And Living Your Dreams

Managing Your Money Post Covid: Financial Management Skills For An Era Of High Inflation And Market Disruption

Retire On Your Own Terms: A Simple Guide To Financially Literate Retirement Planning

Your Ultimate Money Makeover: Manage Your Money Better, Take Control Of Your Finances And Your Life

Teaching Kids Money 101: Simple Parenting Strategies For Raising Financially Literate Kids From Toddler To Teen Years And Beyond

Uncle Ben's Money Lessons: Book I: Do You Want To Work For Money? A Vacation Story With An Adventure Into The World Of Money

Nft Investing 101: A Beginner's Guide To Collectible Digital Assets

Stock Market Investing 101: A Practical Beginners

Guide To Online And Offline Stock Trading

Investing In Etfs 101: A Beginner's Guide For Building Wealth With Exchange-Traded Funds

Day Trading 101: A Complete Beginner's Guide To Trading The Markets

Forex Trading 101: A Beginner's Guide And Strategies To Profitable Currency Trading

Options Trading 101: A Beginner's Guide To Trading Stock Options

Futures Trading 101: A Step-By-Step Guide And Strategies For Beginner Traders

www.ingramcontent.com/pod-product-compliance
Lightning Source LLC
Chambersburg PA
CBHW071914210526
45479CB00002B/410